THE COMMUNICATION GAME

Summary Publications* in the Johnson & Johnson Baby Products Company Pediatric Round Table Series:

Maternal Attachment and Mothering Disorders: A Round Table

Edited by Marshall H. Klaus, M.D.,
         Treville Leger and
         Mary Anne Trause, Ph.D.

Social Responsiveness of Infants

Edited by Evelyn B. Thoman, Ph.D.
         and Sharland Trotter

Learning Through Play

By Paul Chance, Ph.D.

The Communication Game

Edited by Abigail Peterson Reilly, Ph.D.

See Suggestions For Further Reading for listing of counterpart scientific publications.

THE COMMUNICATION GAME

Perspectives on the Development of
Speech, Language and
Non-Verbal Communication Skills

Edited by
Abigail Peterson Reilly, Ph.D.

*Summary of a Pediatric Round Table
Chaired by Rachel E. Stark, Ph.D.,
Director, Hearing and Speech Division,
The John F. Kennedy Institute
Baltimore, Maryland*

Foreword by
Rachel E. Stark, Ph.D.

Sponsored by

Johnson & Johnson
BABY PRODUCTS COMPANY

Library of Congress Cataloging in Publication Data
Main entry under title:

The Communication game.

(Johnson & Johnson Baby Products Company pediatric
round table series; 4)
   1. Interpersonal communication in children — Congresses. 2. Nonverbal communication in children —
Congresses. 3. Children — Language — Congresses. 4.
Language acquisition — Congresses. 5. Communicative
disorders in children — Congresses. 6. Medical screening — Congresses. I. Reilly, Abigail Peterson. II. Series:
Johnson & Johnson Baby Products Company. Johnson &
Johnson Baby Products Company pediatric round table;
4. [DNLM: I. Language development Congresses 2. Non-
verbal communication — In infancy and childhood —
Congresses 3. Speech — In infancy and childhood —
Congresses WS 105.5.C8 C734]
BF723.C57C65   155.4'13   80-83517

ISBN 0-931562-05-8

Printed in the United States of America

214927

To all those whose love for children and fascination with their complexity guide them in their search for a better understanding of the development of human communication.

CONTENTS

PARTICIPANTS

LOIS BLOOM, Ph.D.
Department of Psychology
Teachers College
Columbia University
New York, NY 10027

ARNOLD J. CAPUTE, M.D., F.A.A.P.
Deputy Medical Director
The John F. Kennedy Institute
707 North Broadway
Baltimore, MD 21205

ROBIN S. CHAPMAN, Ph.D.
Department of Communicative Disorders
University of Wisconsin
1975 Willow Drive
Madison, WI 53706

JAMES T. DETTRE
Director of Marketing Services
Johnson & Johnson
Baby Products Company
220 Centennial Avenue
Piscataway, NJ 08854

REBECCA E. EILERS, Ph.D.
Assistant Professor of Pediatrics
  and Psychology
Mailman Center for Child Development
University of Miami
P.O. Box 016820
Miami, FL 33101

ALAN FOGEL, Ph.D.
Department of Child Development
  and Family Studies
Purdue University
West Lafayette, IN 47907

KURT W. FISCHER, Ph.D.
Department of Psychology
University of Denver
University Park
Denver, CO 80208

THOMAS F. GORMAN
Director of Consumer Research
Johnson & Johnson
Baby Products Company
220 Centennial Avenue
Piscataway, NJ 08854

GERALD GRATCH, Ph.D.
Department of Psychology
University of Houston
Houston, TX 77004

JANET B. HARDY, M.D.
Professor of Pediatrics
The Johns Hopkins University
School of Medicine
720 Rutland Avenue
Baltimore, MD 21205

DAVID INGRAM, Ph.D.
Department of Linguistics
The University of British Columbia
2075 Westbrook Mall
Vancouver, B.C.
Canada V6T IW5

JEROME KAGAN, Ph.D.
Professor of Psychology
Department of Psychology
    and Social Relations
Harvard University
William James Hall
33 Kirkland Street
Cambridge, MA 02138

RAYMOND D. KENT, Ph.D.
Senior Research Associate
Human Communication Laboratories
The Boys Town Institute
555 North 30th Street
Omaha, NE 68131

PATRICIA K. KUHL, Ph.D.
Associate Professor
Department of Speech and Hearing
    Science
Child Development and Mental
    Retardation Center, WJ-10
University of Washington
Seattle, WA 98195

LEWIS A. LEAVITT, M.D.
Department of Pediatrics
Waisman Center for Mental Retardation
    and Human Development
University of Wisconsin
1500 Highland Avenue
Madison, WI 53706

KARIN LIFTER, M. PHIL.
Department of Psychology
Teachers College
Columbia University, Box 5
New York, NY 10027

RONALD W. NETSELL, Ph.D.
The Boys Town Institute
555 North 30th Street
Omaha, NE 68131

D. KIMBROUGH OLLER, Ph.D.
Assistant Professor of Pediatrics and
    Psychology
Mailman Center for Child Development
University of Miami
P.O. Box 016820
Miami, FL 33101

D. R. PETTERSON, Ph.D.
Vice President and General Manager
    Professional Products
Johnson & Johnson
Baby Products Company
220 Centennial Avenue
Piscataway, NJ 08854

DIANE J. POWELL, R.N., M.A.
Manager of Professional Relations
Johnson & Johnson
501 George Street
New Brunswick, NJ 08903

ABIGAIL PETERSON REILLY, Ph.D.
Science Writer
43 Fern Street
Hartford, CT 06105

ROBERT B. ROCK, JR., M.A.
Director of Professional Relations
Johnson & Johnson
501 George Street
New Brunswick, NJ 08903

STEVEN SAWCHUK, M.D.
Director, Medical Services and
Chairman, Institute for Pediatric
    Service
Johnson & Johnson
Baby Products Company
220 Centennial Avenue
Piscataway, NJ 08854

RACHEL E. STARK, Ph.D.
Director, Hearing and Speech Division
The John F. Kennedy Institute
707 North Broadway
Baltimore, MD 21205

DANIEL N. STERN, M.D.
Department of Psychiatry
The New York Hospital
Cornell Medical Center
525 East 68th Street
New York, NY 10021

EDWARD TRONICK, Ph.D.
Department of Psychology
The Commonwealth of Massachusetts
University of Massachusetts
Amherst, MA 01003

PETER H. WOLFF, M.D.
The Children's Hospital Medical Center
Enders Research Laboratory
300 Longwood Avenue
Boston, MA 02115

PREFACE

"Language Behavior in Infancy and Early Childhood" was the subject of the fourth in the series of Pediatric Round Tables sponsored by the Johnson & Johnson Baby Products Company. In fostering this series, the company has sought to provide support for a scholarly undertaking which will bring to interested parents and child-health care professionals new concept information and insights at the innovative edge of child development. THE COMMUNICATION GAME, written and edited by Abigail Peterson Reilly, Ph.D., is the summary publication based on the material presented at this fourth Round Table. It has been reviewed and edited by the Round Table Chairperson, Rachel E. Stark, Ph.D., and by the other participating professionals.

In THE COMMUNICATION GAME, Dr. Reilly has distilled much of the rich and thoughtful discussion of the Round Table, opinions of twenty of the world's authorities in the field of communication development. What she has to say reflects the fascination of these authorities with the complexities of communication development and provides insights into their comments and opinions on the unraveling of these complexities. The publication offers new perspectives on non-verbal communication, speech reception and production and the development of language and thought. In the process it focuses attention on language development as an indicator of the presence or absence of a variety of disabilities and the possibility of using language development in developmental screening as a diagnostic tool for predicting the child at risk.

With the publication of this summary volume, the Johnson & Johnson Baby Products Company seeks to offer parents and practitioners in the medical and caretaking fields a timely and useful body of information on the subject of "Language Behavior in Infancy and Early Childhood."

Robert B. Rock, Jr., M.A.
Director of Professional Relations

Foreword

Rachel E. Stark, Ph.D.
Director, Hearing and Speech Division
The John F. Kennedy Institute
Baltimore, Maryland

The purpose of this book is to give professionals who deal with children a better understanding of language development and language disorders. In spite of the growth of our knowledge in these areas over the past 10 or 20 years, many parents who seek professional help because they believe that their children's language is not developing normally are still frequently turned away by pediatricians and others with the advice, "Let us wait and see". It is understandable that physicians, nurses, and other professionals dealing with children have taken this attitude in the past. There is a great deal of variability among normal children with respect to the ages at which they produce their first words, phrases, and sentences. Many late starters catch up with their peers, and at five years of age are on a par with them in their use of language and their ability to learn in school. Others, however, do not catch up. These children may have significant hearing losses or oral motor involvement which, if not recognized early, may lead to unnecessary delays in remediation, to learning problems, and to consequent emotional disturbances and/or low self-esteem in the child. Other children may be retarded or may have severe difficulty in relating to their family members, to teachers or to their peers. If these problems are not managed correctly in the beginning, the cost to the family may be unduly great. How then, can the pediatrician, pediatric nurse professional or otolaryngologist determine whether or not a child has significant problems which are likely to prevent language learning, and is, therefore, at risk for a communication disorder?

One approach is early milestone information about responses to sounds or auditory comprehension, and sound-making or the beginnings of speech. Examples come from the work of Gesell, Cattell, Griffiths, and others. The implementation of a scale of developmental milestones may involve some testing in the pediatrician's office, for example, of responses to sounds, but ratings will very often depend largely on the mother's report. This fact may give rise to some problems, because not all of the terms used in developmental scales are well defined. The term "babbling," for example, has been used quite differently by different workers, and only recently have different levels and types of babbling been differentiated. It has not even been possible for all workers to agree on the definition of the "first word," and thus to say when that milestone is reached in a given child. The ability to say words evolves very gradually from proto-words or pre-words, that is, identifiable sound patterns such as "da," that are used in a very general way to mean "I want that," or "Look at that." These pre-words have to be differentiated from real words which are used to indicate specific objects, such as "doggie," or specific actions, such as "put." It is not always easy to say exactly when word-like sounds or proto-words become real words as we usually understand them. Nor is it easy to differentiate words that are used only a few times and then forgotten, from words that remain in the child's vocabulary and are used frequently. The use of phrases may also be problematic because some, like "Thank you," or "Wanna eat cookie," may not be phrases to the child, but may instead just be very long single words.

Some milestones, such as cooing (that is, making pleasure sounds while smiling at the mother, which begins at six to eight weeks), and the sudden spurt in vocabulary growth which takes place after the first 20 or 30 words are learned (around 18 to 24 months of age), may be more readily identified and unmistakable than others. But milestones of this nature tend to be quite far apart on the developmental scale. In deciding about other, less easily identified milestones, it might be useful to have tape recordings of a range of sounds which are characteristic of a given developmental level. This would help the mother identify those sounds which she is confident are being produced by her baby and those which are not.

A more comprehensive approach to the early identification of communication disorders might be to consider all of the ways in which normal development of language may be disrupted. In other words, what are the component skills that a child must have to learn spoken language? And what are the environmental influences that may foster or impair language acquisition?

A number of aspects of communication are considered in this book. The first section deals with social interaction and its beginnings very early in life. In this section, the early face-to-face interaction of mothers and babies is considered as setting the stage for both verbal and non-verbal communication skills. Non-verbal skills include the body language aspects of gaze, position, and distance from a partner, as well as the messages conveyed by facial expression, tone of voice, loudness of speech, and the use of lively intonation patterns versus monotonous ones.

The second section deals with the development of the mechanisms of speech, that is, the development of mouth parts and the sound source in the larynx, as well as the development of the motor control system by which movements of these parts are coordinated and controlled in speaking. It also deals with the development of listening skills, and of the ability to hear differences between speech sounds such as "ba" and "pa," and to recognize sounds such as "ah" each time they are spoken. This is more difficult than it might seem. When the same sounds are spoken by different people, the utterances are physically different. Differences in the age and/or sex of the speaker, .as well as whether or not the sound is spoken with a rising or falling speech pattern (contour), or when it is spoken in different words, for example in "can" and "far," are all factors which bear on the listener's ability to hear the differences. Indeed it may be hard to see what a number of different "ah's" have in common with one another, even though they sound the same to us as adults.

Finally, in the third section, language is considered in relation to thought. One of the participants says that language is the best predictor of intelligence in children. Indeed it is probable that in most normal children there is a general relationship between language and thought. Thus, a child who is retarded mentally would be expected to learn language more slowly than a normal child, while a highly intelligent child would be expected to use language more effectively than the average child. This is not a hard and fast, one-to-one relationship, however. Language and thought may develop somewhat independently, even in the normal child. Some children who are average or above average in intelligence may be slow to speak, and others who are very talkative or highly imitative in language learning may not be as bright as they seem.

By considering each of these aspects of communication separately, and by considering them in relation to one another, it is possible to identify risk factors or bizarre and unusual behaviors that will complement our use of milestone information in assessing communication skills in children.

The first section of the book explores the manner in which infants learn to take a role in regulating exchanges between themselves and their mothers. These exchanges are regulated jointly by the mother and the baby, but the baby takes a definite role in indicating readiness to communicate, in taking turns, in initiating exchanges and eventually in manipulating the behavior of the adult. What is the significance of a failure to learn these skills in early infancy? The answer to this is not entirely clear. The failure may arise from a lack of interest or of input from the mother, as in the case of some young adolescent parents, or it may be related to a defect in the child's ability to interact. At the same time, problems in both the mother and infant may be implicated. It is suspected, for example, that many of the children who have been neglected, abused or, in extreme cases, locked up in a closet for years, may have been abnormal or difficult to manage in the first place.

The pediatrician should be alert for signs of rejection on the part of the mother toward her baby. The lack of a special kind of talking to the baby is one way this is shown. He should also be alert for signs of lack of responsiveness to the mother on the part of the baby. Some questions he should keep in mind are: Does the baby fail to look at the mother, to attend to the mother or to what she does with objects? Does the infant fail to respond to her voice or to behave differently toward the mother and a stranger? Babies who are colicky, who do not like to be held, or who become upset when adults try to get them to pay attention, may well be at risk for a communication disorder. These children may need special management and special attention to their style of interaction if they are to develop communication skills.

The second section of the book is devoted to studies of the development of speech perception and speech production in children. The effects of hearing loss upon speech perception and speech production skills in young children have long been recognized. It has also been suggested, however, that some children who have normal hearing may nevertheless be much less able than others to process what they hear, and especially to process speech. Some children may have more difficulty in listening to important aspects of speech than others, or may develop these abilities more slowly. The speech signal is one that attracts attention and is highly interesting to normal babies, especially if a special mode of talking called 'motherese' is adopted by the adult. The speech of adults, however, especially when they are talking to one another, is a signal that changes very rapidly over time. It contains sudden on-off sound changes, brief duration noise events and rapidly changing portions. It may be that the ability to make sense of such a rapidly changing signal is learned very slowly by some children who are otherwise normal. It appears that normal infants are born with certain auditory processing capabilities which humans share with other mammals. But the ability to integrate these skills and to make use of them may develop at different rates in different children. Ways of assessing these listening skills are only now being devised for infants. The problem of assessing speech perception skills is made more difficult by the fact that most normal young children appear to understand what is said to them, even when they do not. They appear to understand because they have a habit of attending to their mothers and are often able to make very good guesses at what it is the mother expects them to do, even when they are not processing more than a word or two of what she actually says. This very fact, however, should alert the pediatrician to pay attention to any complaint from a mother that a young child does not understand her, or that s/he seems to take a long time to figure out what she is saying.

Speech motor skills may be delayed or disturbed in children who have cerebral palsy or oral facial anomalies, such as cleft palate. Speech motor skills have been assessed by observing feeding behavior in young children, and also by noting the sounds they produce. The contributors to the second section of the book point out that these two activities are not necessarily related. If a young child has a severe problem in swallowing, biting, or chewing, and if he drools excessively in the second year of life, then it is likely that he will also have trouble with talking. However, though talking and eating may share a final common path in the motor system, the young child may have a higher-level problem of speech motor control which is not accompanied by feeding difficulty. It is important for the pediatrician to note reports on both feeding problems and any failure to make consonant sounds in babbling, or in attempts to produce words. The lack of consonant sounds may be a sign of a speech motor disorder. In addition, the failure to make consonant sounds at the ends of words, if it persists well into the second or third year of life, may be a sign of speech motor difficulty.

In the section on language and thought, it is suggested that some aspects of language may be more closely related to thought than others. The meanings that children express and the content of what they say is more likely to reflect the level of their intelligence and what they know, than the way in which they express them. The ability to organize sentences and to develop grammar may not be as closely related to intelligence. Grammatical development may be related to auditory processing skills or imitative abilities in some children. It is important, however, in thinking about grammatical development, to consider both comprehension and production of spoken language by children. Although traditionally it has been held that comprehension comes before production in development, it turns out that that is not quite correct. Apparent comprehension, that is, responding to the gestures and to the intonation patterns of the mother as well as to her speech, and using guesswork based on an ongoing situation does indeed often come before production of language. But in comprehension, the young child understands only what he already knows, and what is already present in a situation in front of him. He cannot understand what is said to him outside of that immediate experience. In production, on the other hand, the child talks about novel or unusual aspects of the situation he is in, or indicates the one thing that is not already obvious in that situation. It is not, therefore, safe to assume that a child who uses language well necessarily understands fully what he is saying, or understands language addressed to him at the same level of grammatical complexity. It is also important to carefully and critically assess the child's comprehension of language, before deciding that there is a significant gap between comprehension and production of speech.

There are two themes woven through the various sections of this book, and it is important that both be considered in any assessment of a child's language development. The first theme is individual differences among children, and the second is connectivity versus discontinuity in development.

Individual differences are important because young children may take very different paths to the common goal of speaking a language. If a behavior is considered to be a milestone which, in fact, is subject to a great deal of individual variation, then it may lead us badly astray in our assessment. Milestones in all of the traditional developmental scales are designed to capture commonalities of development and not individual differences. As time goes on, new milestones or new stages of development are proposed and outlined. But this can lead to problems too, because aspects of development that are not found in all children, or that may occur in different sequential orders in different children, may creep in. Assessment based on scales such as these might again lead us into error.

The notions of connectivity and discontinuity are also important in assessment. These terms refer to behaviors that are found in early periods of development and then reappear at later periods of development, at which time they may be used quite differently. An example is reflexive walking, which is found in the newborn infant. If the newborn is held upright with his feet in contact with a level surface, he will exhibit reflexive walking movements. These resemble the movements of true walking which the infant learns at 11 to 12 months of age. Reflexive walking disappears after a month or so, unless an experimenter maintains it artificially. What is the connection of reflexive walking with real walking? Is there any connection? If the infant were unable to engage in reflexive walking because of some outside interference, for example, because his legs were in casts, would it matter? Would he still walk normally at the usual time?

While questions such as these are of theoretical interest, they are also of practical importance to the pediatrician. Their importance revolves around issues of prediction. We know that early measures of development are not always predictive of later development, except perhaps in extreme cases (for example, of profound retardation). This lack of predictive power may be due to errors of measurement. It may also, however, be related to another consideration. Is early reflexive walking predictive of later walking or not? Is babbling predictive of talking? The answer may be that if the reflexive or more primitive behaviors are not produced under favorable circumstances, or cannot be elicited, then the appearance of the later forms of that behavior may be delayed. If, on the other hand, the earlier behaviors are observed at the normal time, the emergence of the later behaviors may not necessarily be guaranteed. The later versions of walking, gesturing and speaking may represent new combinations of behaviors which include the early walking, pointing or babbling. If, however, other components of these later behaviors, for example, righting reflexes in true walking, appreciation of means to an end in pointing, or auditory processing abilities in speech, are delayed or deviant, then the development of the more mature behavior may not be possible. Alternatively, failure of the integration of the simpler components into new patterns of behavior may be related to overall developmental delay.

The questions about assessment which are raised in this book are important for the pediatrician, pediatric nurse practitioner and other professionals in their initial screening of children at risk for communication problems. They are also important for the more indepth evaluations carried out by other specialists in the team. Children who are considered to be delayed or deviant should be referred to such specialists, that is, to the psychologist, the speech/language pathologist or the audiologist. These professionals must examine communication problems in greater detail. Then, working with the team, they must decide what course of action will be most beneficial to the child. Some things to be considered are whether compensatory strategies may be helpful to the child, whether a technical aid or support will be of value, or whether adjustment of expectations, or ways of handling the child's problem on the part of the family will be most effective—or indeed if all of the above should be tried. Unless these questions can be answered quickly and accurately, valuable resources may be wasted, the resources of the professional team, the resources of the family, and most important of all, the resource of the child. We believe that the studies described in this book are important for these endeavors, and that they all suggest new approaches to assessment and ultimately to treatment of communication problems in children.

INTRODUCTION

How does the young child learn to communicate? What do we know about the development of speech, language and non-verbal skills in normal children that will help us to identify and habilitate the handicapped child?

The papers summarized in this book represent some of the latest efforts to answer these questions. The majority of this research focuses on describing normal communication development. Understanding the similarities and differences among normally developing children is a necessary foundation upon which to build the ability to identify the child who is not developing normally, and to plan therapy programs to meet the needs of such a child.

Unfortunately, it is widely believed that normal development covers such a wide range of individual differences that early signs of significant deviations in development sometimes go unnoticed, or are dismissed as unimportant. This may have serious consequences for the child and his family. On the other hand, no one would suggest that all children are identical in development. It is as important to recognize individuality in development as it is to identify significant deviations from the norm.

It is hoped that the reader will find the information presented here to be a valuable aid in understanding the various aspects of communication development—non-verbal communication, speech comprehension and production, and the development of language and thought. The reader will not, however, find universal agreement among the contributors. The conference upon which this publication is based was rich in thoughtful and concerned differences of opinion among the participants. What they shared was fascination with the complexities of communication development, and dedication to the task of unraveling these complexities.

A logical next step is to use this research to develop better and more reliable means for assessing the development of communication skills. It is hoped that professionals and parents will find in this volume the inspiration to modify and supplement their familiar routines in ways which will better serve the needs of children.

Chapter I
INFANT NON-VERBAL COMMUNICATION

(Discussant: Peter H. Wolff, M.D.)

The papers included in this section describe non-verbal, social communication development and related aspects of physical development in infants and very young children. While it is not common to find these topics included when speech and language development are being discussed, it is clear from the content of these papers that infants learn some very important rules about communicating in a social context, and learn them very early in development.

In the first paper, Edward Tronick points out that infants have remarkable capacities for adjusting and regulating their own behavior. In social interactions, babies respond appropriately to adult behavior, appear to follow the communication rule of taking turns, and produce novel behaviors depending on the situation. This early ability to establish a social relationship is apparently not learned, but is a natural, inborn capacity of the human infant.

Daniel Stern describes the various behaviors which infants use to signal that they are ready to interact. These signals seem to be used in almost adult ways as soon as the child is physically capable of producing them. Stern suggests that the child's readiness to communicate affects the meaning of communicative acts, and should be taken into account in studying language development. Suggestions are also offered as to why some early non-verbal behaviors are eventually replaced by verbal equivalents, and others are not.

"Too early" gestures are the topic of Alan Fogel's presentation. These are gestures, produced by the infant, which resemble non-verbal signals used by older children and adults. What is the purpose of these gestures for the infant? Fogel suggests a number of explanations, some of which are directly related to later verbal development.

The final paper in this section provides an additional perspective for understanding the nature and meaning of early gestures. Arnold Capute and his co-authors present a description of primitive reflexes—movement patterns which are present in the newborn and gradually disappear. Primarily concerned with developing a clinical screening tool for identifying children with abnormal motor development, these developmental pediatricians also point out that early gestures are probably purely reflexive. If so, they may not have the kind of communicative significance suggested by Tronick, Stern and Fogel.

Peter Wolff of the Children's Hospital Medical Center in Boston discussed the Tronick, Stern and Fogel papers and their relationship to speech and language development. He pointed out that the formal aspects of language have usually been studied without taking social context into account. There has been no concern with the development of "communicative competence" as a pre-requisite for language acquisition; little study of the infant's use of words prior to the stage of putting two or more words together; and little concern about non-verbal, vocal utterances as a preparation for later language development. At the same time, however, the term "communicative competence" is very vague, and can be used to cover any social signal or behavior pattern that might be interpreted as a signal by the social partner. Therefore, "communicative competence" is not a very useful idea unless its operations are better defined. Wolff pointed out that current thinking about the relationship between studies of non-verbal behavior and of language development is based on one of two assumptions. The first assumption is that there must be some basic minimum of social interaction or else language will not develop. Babies who grow up in total isolation don't speak. This appears to be quite obvious, but we don't know what the basic required minimum of social interaction is.

A corollary of this assumption is that severe deprivation or isolation (rather than total isolation) in some way affects language development. Yet even in extreme cases such as the Wild Boy of Aveyron, or Genie who is said to have been kept in a closet for 12 years, there is a strong bias toward language development, even under bizarre conditions. Some of these severely isolated children eventually developed limited, functional verbal communication skills. (The effects of isolation, however, have to be considered in relation to the possibility that these children had abnormal behaviors or, in the case of the "Wild Boy", mental retardation, in the first place. *Ed.*)

One problem is that we don't know what aspects of language might be affected in a child who is totally isolated, since there may be hidden effects as well as immediately obvious ones. Children raised in reasonably good institutions with multiple caretakers, and handicapped children—deaf, blind, and thalidomide babies— also have very disordered early social experiences in some ways, but may become competent speakers, nevertheless. This is further support of the idea that there is a strong tendency toward the development of at least functional communication skills in children. It also suggests that rather powerful inborn capacities appear to be present in the human infant, and that these require a minimum of environmental stimulation to develop. The tendency for children to acquire language is an adaptive capacity that can reach an end point, by various pathways. What is unknown is the exact nature of the end point, what "drives" the child toward it, and what is the range of alternative pathways to the same end state.

The second major idea which stimulates investigation of early mother-child interaction, Wolff said, is that, given a basic minimum of social contact, subtle variation in the amount of interaction, sensitivity, or responsiveness between mother and child will in some way eventually affect certain aspects of language performance. While these claims have not been confirmed, there is now some evidence that variations in the details of mother-infant interaction will have an effect on certain aspects of language performance. The richness of the child's vocabulary, the grammatical complexity of sentences spoken, or the expression of complex meanings by the child may be affected. Wolff posed a key question: How necessary, to what purpose, and with respect to which features of language is early experience important? For the most part this appears to be a totally open question.

If variations of verbal communication do, in fact, depend on subtle variations in mother-infant interaction, on face-to-face-contact and so on, then a further question is: What difference do social transactions make? The studies which claim that there is a relationship between early infant-mother social interaction and later language development are frequently conducted in a laboratory using middle-class, white American children and their parents. These families are not representative of the population, and the interactions between these mothers and children may not be typical of what goes on in everyday life in most families. Furthermore, the main emphasis in these studies is on the interaction between *mother* and infant. We do not know much about interaction between the infant and his/her father or siblings. Finally, Wolff noted, there has been little follow-up to demonstrate the effect of early social interaction on any aspect of later language development, to demonstrate, in other words, that the observed effects are anything more than transient phenomena which have very little consequence for language competence in later childhood.

The four papers in Section I should be read in relationship to one another, and to the ideas expressed by Wolff, in order to arrive at a balanced view of many of the factors contributing to early communication development.

Infant Communicative Intent

Edward Tronick, Ph.D.

Communicative intentions are generally not ascribed to infants prior to the age of 7 or 8 months by most workers interested in language or in theories of cognition. At that age, objects come to be incorporated into the communication setting. However, when the infant is observed in face-to-face interaction, it is clear that with behaviors such as smiling and vocalizing, even the 3- to 4-month-old infant is attempting to communicate with his/her partner.

There is a sequence of tasks during infancy. During the newborn period, the infant's task is to regulate sleeping, feeding, quieting and arousing. The infant accomplishes this task by coordinating internal processes, such as digestion, with the timing of events in the environment such as caretaking, feeding, diapering. (Infants lacking in or showing poor internal organization often have developmental disorders.) This development of complicated, organized behavior is dependent on built-in timing mechanisms which make the coordination possible. But the infant's daily cycles of sleeping, waking and the like are also influenced by the caretaking routines in the home and the particular person carrying them out. When either the routine or the person is changed, the infant's pattern changes. Thus, the infant is capable of goal-directed action adapted to a specific situation, such as the caretaking routine.

Beginning at about 2 months of age, the infant is able to take a more active role in exchanges, usually between the mother and himself/herself. The infant begins to actively regulate interacting during caretaking and face-to-face encounters. It was this stage Tronick concentrated upon. He found that if the *interaction* is defined as *that which is regulated by the infant's actions,* it becomes clear that the infant has striking capacities for intentional communication during such interchanges. Joint regulation of interactions requires that the mother and the baby share communicative goals, the meaning of their communicative acts and the rules governing their sequencing. In trying to understand the communicative capacities of the infant and the prerequisites for language development, we must determine the extent to which the infant is able to modify his/her communicative acts, and describe the rules that govern these acts.

Wolff described built-in regulators of serial order in infants—central nervous system mechanisms that cannot be explained by experience alone. It is this central organization which permits the occurrence of coordinated interchanges between mothers and infants at 2 to 4 months, and even during the newborn period.

Brazelton, Koslowski, and Main described rhythmic cycles of attention and non-attention in the infant during face-to-face interactive exchanges. Mothers and infants were able to fit their cycles together. Stern called the positive segments of face-to-face interactions "games" in which mothers and infants were able to coordinate both gaze and vocalizations. Tronick observed that most of the shifts from one kind of interchange, e.g. play, to another kind, e.g. talk, took place simultaneously for mother and child even as young as 3 months of age—an amazing degree of coordination. Developmentally from 3 to 9 months there was a steady increase in the amount of total interaction time during which both partners were engaged in the same type of interactive play. At 2 months, an alternating sequence of mother vocalization and infant pausing could be observed. Such an interaction was a coordinated sequence of joint behaviors. These sequences were organized within several timing patterns which lasted from tenths of a second to several seconds. These timing patterns were nested, with the smaller units grouped within the larger units in a hierarchical fashion.

These observations lead us to ask: Is the infant able to adjust and modify his/her behavior in response to that of the caretaker, or is it the caretaker who is responsible for the coordination? To answer this question, we must show that the infant's behavior occurs only in a given type of situation, and that it is appropriate to that situation. Several studies have shown that the infant is able to discriminate between different kinds of situations and to act appropriately in social and non-social situations. Bullowa contrasted the infant's behavior when s/he was alone and when s/he was with a person. She found that when interacting with the mother, the infant cooperated with her in complicated interactional sequences, but when the infant was alone, s/he had only a small repertoire of behaviors.

Brazelton and his colleagues compared the behavior of infants dealing with objects with their behavior when interacting with people. With objects, the infants focused attention for up to two minutes without any shift of gaze, then "pounced" at the object. They exhibited intense facial expressions, and made jerky movements. With a person, infants showed cycles of attention toward the person and then away from the person four to five times per minute.

Movements were smooth and more like gestures; facial expressions varied and included smiles. Further, Ricks, Krafchuk, and Tronick found that at 3 months, most interaction time was in face-to-face play; at 6 months, more than 40 percent of the interaction time was spent focused on objects; and at 9 months, the interaction consisted of elaborated sequences in which play with objects and forms of face-to-face play were combined. Infants also modified their behavior so that it was appropriate to the quality and kind of behavior presented by an initially unfamiliar adult. Even at 3 months of age, the infant acted differently with mother, father, and stranger.

Tronick described a number of studies in which mothers were asked to behave in a number of different, sometimes unusual ways, and the reactions of the babies were observed. When mothers held a frozen posture and a still face while looking toward their infants, the babies looked away and eventually slumped away with a hopeless facial expression. Cohn found that infants reacted to mothers acting in a completely unemotional way with initial wariness and made sounds and gestures which seemed to be designed to produce some kind of response from the mother. The infants eventually cried when these attempts failed. Als found that when the mother was presented in profile, the baby reached out and made calling sounds. When the pace of an exchange was slowed down, the infant showed more positive affect. When mothers acted in a jerky, puppet-like fashion, the infants stared at them in a fascinated way for long periods of time as if the mother were an object rather than a person.

These results cannot be explained either by proposing that the babies were responding to the novelty of the mothers' behavior, or that the babies were simply aroused by the mothers' behavior. In these studies, it appeared that the babies responded in a specific way to a particular set of behaviors or lack of behaviors from the mother. Similar effects have been demonstrated in naturalistic observations. Brazelton and his colleagues showed that when mothers overload their infants with too many behaviors too fast and do not allow the infant to take its turn, the infant looks away from the mother. Massie analyzed home movies of infants taken prior to their eventual diagnosis of childhood psychosis at 3 to 4 years of age, and found similar distorted patterns of interactions even when the mothers were not overloading the infant. The mothers would often fail to respond appropriately to the infant's signals, and in their exchanges they would be completely out of phase with one another.

Different patterns can also be seen when mother or infant is blind. Adamson and colleagues studied the sighted infant of blind parents. The blind mother had a characteristically expressionless, immobile face, to which the infant responded by turning away. Despite this, the infant developed normally by eventually finding ways to interact with the mother which were quite similar in structure to those of babies with seeing parents, but without using face-to-face positioning. In other words, the use of gazing at one another was distorted so that other modes of communication could be employed. With sighted adults, the normal baby switched and interacted in a typical face-to-face fashion. It has also been reported that a blind infant of sighted parents was able to develop normal communication using hearing and touch to gain information from the social environment and to control his/her own interactive behaviors. Thus, apparently, no particular modes or senses are of unique importance to the infant during this developmental period. Different ways of generating communication signals can be used in order to establish satisfactory exchanges with adults. Based on this information, we can draw a number of conclusions:

1. Infants are able to modify their behavior appropriately during social interaction;
2. when the interaction is distorted, the infant engages in behaviors that are aimed at reinstating the normal interactions;
3. when they do not succeed, the infants become distressed;
4. the infant's goal is to establish mutual exchanges;
5. rules of interaction are built into the infant; and
6. the infant regulates the interaction as well as the mother. This is most evident during distorted interactions, in which the infant acts to change things

and establish a more normal exchange again.

A central question is: Why does the infant regulate interactions? Joint coordination of tasks is a fundamental human adaptation. The ability to coordinate an interaction, to share a goal of mutual exchange, is a prerequisite to coordinating another person's behavior with a goal related to an outside event or object.

There are strong indications that the initial ability to establish a social relationship is not learned. In normal interaction, even in the newborn, there are too many complicated patterns of exchange involving mothers, infants, and other adults for the infant to have been able to learn each of those patterns in such a short span of time. In addition, it appears that each interaction is unique. Each is created at the time of occurrence, and the infant often appears to be producing new behaviors which s/he has not experienced from others or exhibited before. In this sense, the infant's interactive ability is similar to the later skill in language of producing a novel utterance which s/he has not heard before.

In order to accomplish joint regulation of behavior, the infant has as his/her goal interacting in a particular fashion. This goal must be communicated to and shared with a partner, usually the child's mother. Therefore, some channels for receiving and sending information must be functioning from very early in life. The sequence of the communication behavior of infant and partner follows rules of taking turns, and of acting simultaneously. Furthermore, the infant appears to possess these rules when s/he is born without having to learn them. They are innate.

The available data suggest that infants have the capacity to deal with objects and also to manipulate adults before they are able to deal with objects and with adults in social interaction at the same time. Thus, they first deal with or refer to interactive behaviors in which they themselves participate. Since referring to jointly regulated behavior and referring to objects are developmentally distinct, it is important in describing infant development to take both into account. It follows that we should be concerned about the richness of early events, and should avoid focusing only on later developmental accomplishments.

Infant Signals of Readiness to Communicate

Daniel N. Stern, M.D.

During infancy, children develop a set of non-verbal behaviors which determine whether communication can begin or continue, and what kinds of communication can occur. These behaviors are gaze, head orientation, body orientation, position in space, posture and distance. How do these signals develop?

Communicative readiness does not mean only that the inattentiveness of one partner demands attention-getting behaviors by the other, or that both partners are paying attention to the same things and information can then be exchanged. These two situations are actually the opposite ends of a spectrum of communicative readiness, along which there are many distinct and important divisions. The infant's degree of readiness to communicate is important because it provides the framework for non-verbal and/or verbal communication.

When mothers and infants spend time together, they affect each other's readiness to interact. This is a predominant feature of their communication. We have observed that much of the time, the infant is more or less not ready to interact. Not only is s/he attending elsewhere, but s/he is actually signalling that s/he is *not* ready by ignoring or refusing attempts by a partner to communicate. Thus, when the mother makes an attempt to communicate, its effect will be different depending upon the child's relative state of readiness at that moment. The infant's readiness state will determine whether the mother's communication is taken at face value, or as an attempt to manipulate the infant's readiness. Readiness is therefore a very important aspect of early communication situations, because it affects their meaning.

In general, the signals of communicative readiness are mutual gaze and vis-à-vis position of the head and body, plus close distance. Movements which indicate the opposite—unreadiness to interact—are gaze aversion, turning the head aside or down, angling the body away from the partner, and moving backwards. It is difficult to generalize about these signals. However, in the mother-infant play situation, we are left with the impression that the major goal is to communicate, or to teach communication. Signals of readiness to communicate probably have evolved from signals of readiness to interact towards other biological goals, such as aggression or sex, for example.

WHEN CAN INFANTS PERFORM THE BEHAVIORS WHICH SIGNAL READINESS TO COMMUNICATE? Infants seem to be able to use these behaviors as soon as they are physically capable of performing them. For example, as soon as an infant can walk, s/he appears to walk toward or away from a partner in order to regulate interpersonal distance. In other words, learning to walk and using this skill to regulate interpersonal spatial relationships seem to go hand in hand. A similar situation exists with respect to the orienting and spatial behaviors we have identified as signals of communication readiness.

GAZE The infant has essentially mature voluntary control of gaze behaviors by the 4th month of life and, at roughly the same time, begins to use gaze to initiate, maintain, terminate and avoid interactions.

HEAD ORIENTATION A surprisingly mature signal system using the head is already in place by 6 months of age. The neck muscles controlling head orientation are among the first to come under voluntary control. From the 3rd to the 6th month, infants seek and greatly enjoy what is usually called face-to-face play. Several distinct spatial and orientational behaviors seem to have different functions:

    gaze and head aversion to the side with head lowered is a "stop" signal;

    gaze and head aversion to the side with head raising and looking up is a "hold" signal;

    head aversion past 100° from the target is a sign of escape or withdrawal;

    head aversion that loses form perception but maintains peripheral vision is seen as a form of monitoring in a partial cut-off position;

    full face-to-face orientation with a glazed look is a different form of unreadiness to interact.

UPPER BODY   Between 5 and 12 months, a number of motor landmarks have been achieved: control of sitting postures; coordination and voluntary control of the upper extremities; crawling and cruising. Used together, these give the child control over the spatial orientation of his/her body. During this period the infant's preference for the human face, voice and touch changes to an interest in objects, and playing with objects on the floor with mother. The infant can now control his/her orientation towards the adult. S/he has more control over indicating readiness to interact, and can also control whether the interactions will be object-oriented or purely interpersonal.

LOWER BODY   With the onset of walking, the full set of non-verbal readiness signals available to adults is available to the infant. Major signals of readiness are functioning by 3 years of age, and change little over the following two years.

FREE PLAY AT 12 MONTHS   When a mother and a 12-month-old infant were observed for 1 minute and 40 seconds during free play, the infant produced at least 12 distinct body movements to establish his readiness to communicate. In this particular example, the partners were in partial conflict: their states of readiness to communicate were different. There were, however, moments of mutual readiness to communicate with shared attention during which information about objects was exchanged. It is these shared situations that are isolated for study in inquiries about language development. However, in ongoing natural interactions, communicative readiness is constantly changing. When negotiation of readiness to communicate is the primary issue, verbal behaviors become secondary. The study of language should include observation of language behaviors in these various contexts.

WHY ARE SIGNALS OF READINESS TO COMMUNI-CATE NON-VERBAL?   Some non-verbal behaviors carried out by young babies are labeled forerunners of language because they are later replaced by their equivalent in words. For example, behaviors such as pointing or reaching for an object may eventually be replaced by a verbal request for the object. After that has occurred, the original non-verbal behaviors may disappear or remain only as accompaniments to the central verbal message. However, many pre-linguistic non-verbal behaviors are never replaced by the formal language system. They appear to be "resistant" to encoding in words. Reaching for an object will fairly soon be replaced by "Gimme." On the other hand, stepping back half a step from another person, averting gaze to the side and lowering the head will never undergo a similar change into words.

WHY DOESN'T FORMAL LANGUAGE COMPLETELY REPLACE THE NON-VERBAL SYSTEM? Our responses to these non-verbal behaviors probably involve the biological level of arousal and the activation of emotions immediately and directly. These behaviors are also ideally designed to communicate dimensional information rather than categorical information. For example, for audible signals, varying emotional levels are expressed by altering the loudness, pitch, stress and speed of what is said. Likewise, head and body orientation and distance are varied so as to provide information concerning which point along a dimension the communication in question occupies.

Non-verbal signals transmit more precise gradient information than verbal ones. In adult verbal communication, what usually occurs is that a general "ball park" level is indicated by the verbal message, and the finetuning is accomplished by the non-verbal behavior. In fact, with conventional messages such as "Hello" or "Oh, really", once the conventional has been observed, virtually all of the information is in *how* it is said, that is, in the dimensional aspect.

Behaviors which resist being put into words also involve signals which can be denied. Speakers need to express hostility, challenge the competence of others or express friendliness and affection in a way that can be denied if they are held to account for it. The surest way to keep a behavior deniable is to prevent it from becoming part of the formal language system.

Readiness to communicate cannot simply be treated as an issue of getting and maintaining attention. It actually constitutes a high order of interpersonal context, and influences the meaning of the language forms used within that context. There is a great need for accurate developmental description of infants' non-verbal communication skills, since many children who will develop disturbed language will also develop disturbances in other forms of communication. By focusing on the entire repertoire of non-verbal communication behaviors, we may be better able to identify and intervene earlier in cases of deviant development.

Gestural Communication During the First Six Months

Alan Fogel, Ph.D.

In human infants, some patterns of movement appear early and remain throughout the life span, for example, the "walking reflex" which can be observed in newborns and disappears in about a month. Our goal is to examine some of the movements made by infants under 6 months, movements which resemble later pre-verbal and verbal communication.

First, let us take a look at some *psychosocial milestones of development.*

Infants have been observed smiling, crying, gazing, grasping, reaching and pointing. Two important questions are: What is the significance of these movements? and Is there continuity between these movements and the gestures used by adults? We observed a number of infants and mothers during a period of 6 months. As they matured, the infants spent less and less time attending to the mother if she was not acting expressively. At the same time, the mothers increased their expressive activity during those times when their babies were attentive. A change in the pattern of taking the initiative was also noted. At 6 weeks of age, the infants waited until the mother made some gesture before responding; at 6 months, the children initiated as many mutual exchanges as their mothers did.

AGE	MILESTONE
2 weeks	Transition from reflex and autonomic activity to less reflexive but still diffuse responses to external stimuli. Response to quantity of stimulation, rather than quality.
8 weeks	Maintains eye contact, control of gaze and head direction. Begins to act on the environment. Smile. Wariness. Quality of stimulation more important than quantity. Prefers familiar objects and people to unfamiliar ones. Eye contact with mother. Face-to-face interaction with adults. Social encounters with mother do not include objects or other people.
4 months	Ability to reach and grasp objects. Attention directed more toward inanimate objects. Parent discouraged because objects become the primary focus of attention. Parent-infant relationship regains its earlier sharing quality during the succeeding year.

We have also studied more than 100 well-defined infant movement patterns such as pointing and grasping. We did not see a clear developmental progression in these movement patterns. However, it is important to mention that the large number of movements we cataloged is much greater than the few behaviors which have usually been used as developmental milestones.

What is the function of these various behaviors? Three-month-olds respond differentially to a wide variety of social situations. They react differently to their mother's voice than to that of a strange female adult. They behave differently when presented with a baby of the same age, a mirror or a doll. At this age also, the infant acts differently when a face-to-face interaction is terminated. It has been shown, for example, that if the interaction was between the infant and the mother, when she leaves the room the infant is more likely to cry, to reach out after her, or look back toward the door. If, on the other hand, the interaction was with an adult female stranger, there is little activity directed toward her when she leaves. Instead, there are general signs of anxiety such as yawning and stereotyped movements of the mouth. We might say that the infants were not simply responding to the stimulus—the adult leaving—but to the prior interaction. This suggests that memory and even emotional factors may play a role in determining which behavior is expressed.

Brazelton and his colleagues asked mothers to keep their faces very still. At first the infants tried to get the mother to react, but eventually turned away and withdrew. Were these babies responding solely to the change in the mother's facial expression? The results of an experiment designed to answer this question showed that the infants did not get upset until the mother returned to her normal facial expression. It seems that the babies remembered how the mother usually behaved, and did not simply respond to whatever facial expression was present at a given time.

It is not clear whether these behaviors are attempts by the infant to communicate. Some think that evolution has provided the baby with behaviors designed to attract the attention and concern of adults; that it is only through association that these early movements take on communicative meaning. On the other hand, infants do take social initiatives by 6 months of age, at least by anticipating a particular kind of response from an adult. Even 3-month-olds begin to expect certain social actions from others, and show that they are upset when the desired event does not take place.

ARE EARLY MOVEMENT PATTERNS BUILT IN TO THE INFANT'S NERVOUS SYSTEM? DO THEY PROVIDE THE ADULT WITH INFORMATION ABOUT THE INFANT'S INTERNAL STATE? This interpretation says that the mother has social skills and intentions, but that the infant does not. It may be that these patterns of movement serve a more direct function for the infant which is not necessarily related to social interaction. Anytime there is movement, there is proprioceptive feedback (awareness of stimulations within the tissues of the body). The muscles and joints involved in the movement automatically send signals to the brain. Could it be that some of these "too early" gestures serve to create *internal* experiences as the basis for later interactions with people and objects in the environment?

In talking to mothers, we have discovered that they notice very little of the large repertoire of their infant's activity. They are taken by expression of strong emotions, but are mostly unaware of more subtle hand and finger movements. Many of these movements become noticed when they actually become expressions of intentions, but not at this early age.

Early motor behaviors are probably tied directly to internal sensations and experiences. It seems that when a baby makes a certain movement, s/he is experiencing something which is related to the event or object which triggered that movement. For example, the sight of an object may attract the baby to the object and cause him/her to grasp at the object. These initial feelings of attraction may become detached from the grasping movement itself, and eventually become the basis for further exploration and awareness of the object. As the infant develops, reaching toward the mother may occur less frequently because it has served its initial function of "getting the infant attracted to the mother", after which the infant develops other more sophisticated and elaborate means of communication.

Pointing may also reflect feelings of attraction. It seems to refer to an object, and it isolates and locates the object in time, space, and experience. At the same time it presents the object to the mother. Pointing in young infants could reflect the experience of recognition, or an interest in features of the environment which are novel.

Most of the early patterns of movement we have observed look like actions which serve some purpose later in infancy: reaching, grasping, pointing, mouthing. When they first appear, they do not seem to serve any clear purpose, and they do not seem intentional. Mothers hardly notice these patterns of movement at this early stage. Embryologists have suggested that patterns of behavior which appear "too early" may serve important functions for the baby which bear little relation to the mature form of the behavior. We suggest that these early-appearing forms may generate feedback which motivates the young infant to attend to potentially important features of the environment.

Primitive Reflexes and Non-Verbal Language in Infancy

Arnold J. Capute, M.D., Bruce K. Shapiro, M.D., Frederick B. Palmer, M.D., Pasquale J. Accardo, M.D., and Renee C. Wachtel, M.D.

Primitive reflexes are movement patterns which initially develop before birth, are present in the newborn, and are readily elicited during the first 6 months as the central nervous system matures. Abnormalities of primitive reflexes may be followed by abnormal motor development, such as failure of the righting and equilibrium responses to develop in the second 6 months, as they normally do. In cerebral palsied patients, reflexes persist to an excessive degree and far beyond the normal time of disappearance.

There is a need to define primitive reflexes in a clinically useful fashion. Several studies have attempted to relate primitive reflexes to later motor outcome. But in fact, little is known about infants with minor deviations, and less is known about the relationship between reflexes and the development of motor function in children. We are presently studying the development of seven primitive reflexes and their interrelationships. A profile of these seven reflexes is being graded on a 5-point scale in an effort to develop a standardized motor screening tool which can be used with children from birth to 2 years of age. With such a tool, the early identification of several groups of children may be possible:

- children whose profile is not normal and thus are at "high risk" for motor involvement;

- children who demonstrate a constellation of reflexes which may make the development of a specific motor act difficult or impossible;

- children who have cerebral palsy; and

- children who have mild brain damage which manifests itself as some form of learning disability.

The seven primitive reflexes being studied are:

the Moro Reflex (M)
the Galant Reflex (G)
the Tonic Labyrinthine Reflex - Supine and -Prone (TLS, TLP)
the Asymmetric Tonic Neck Reflex (ATNR)
the Symmetric Tonic Neck Reflex (STNR)
the Positive Supporting Reflex (PS)
Segmental Rolling (SR).

Initial findings on the first 120 children are related to walking. Children who are walking earlier have primitive reflexes that disappear sooner; those who are late walkers have primitive reflexes which persist.

Non-verbal or gestural communication in early infancy is also being studied in relation to mother-child interaction. A complete knowledge of primitive reflexes is essential to prevent misinterpretations of the movements of the arms and hands. Those studying the gestures of young infants need to be aware that movements of the arms and legs are greatly influenced by the position of the head. At this early age, the infant is "locked into" automatic responses. For example, the asymmetric tonic neck reflex (ATNR), or "fencing reflex", is determined by the baby's head position, with extension of the arm and leg on the chin side and flexion of the arm and leg on the opposite side. One might easily misinterpret a visible ATNR for a willful pushing away of the mother.

The tonic labyrinthine reflex - supine also determines the position of the extremities. If the neck is extended, the shoulders are automatically pulled back and the trunk and legs thrust forward. In some babies this may be interpreted as moving away from the mother. Thus, a damaged baby with excessive reflexes may be seen as "rejecting" if the true reflexive nature of the movement is not understood. In studying finger, hand or arm movements during the first 3 months of life, the head should be in the neutral midline position to minimize the effects of primitive reflexes.

The baby's overall state is also of importance in assessing early gestures. In the Moro reflex the arms are extended to the side and somewhat bent at the elbows, wrists, and fingers, with each thumb and second finger forming a "C" position. A sudden noise may well stimulate the Moro response. While this posture has been interpreted as an attempt to embrace the mother in reaction to a frightening stimulus, the voluntary nature of this "embrace" is questionable.

Early gesture language must be interpreted within the context of overall motor development. Voluntary motor control begins with head and eye movements, followed by head movements in combination with the arms and hands, and finally involves the torso and the legs. Thus, it is essential that the study of communication during early infancy take into account the intimate relationship between speech and language development, and other aspects of the development of the child.

Chapter II
THE DEVELOPMENT OF SPEECH COMPREHENSION AND PRODUCTION

(Discussant: Lewis A. Leavitt, M.D.)

In considering how infants develop the capacity to understand the speech that they hear, it is important to remember that the speech signal which reaches the ear is a complex pattern of sounds produced by a human being. Auditory comprehension is a term which represents the multitude of capacities through which we make sense of these sound patterns. One basic skill is the ability to discriminate one sound from another. From an early age, infants are able to do this—to show that they can hear that *pa* and *ba* are not the same. Is the baby born with this capacity, or does s/he learn to do this by listening to people talk?

Rebecca Eilers and William Gavin discuss a number of important issues in auditory comprehension, and propose a description of the comprehension process which takes inborn abilities and environmental effects into account. They also describe three current methods of testing infant speech perception, one of which may be a valuable clinical tool. This is the Visually Reinforced Infant Speech Discrimination method which provides a reliable assessment of the abilities of individual children to receive and understand audible signals.

In order to make sense out of the sounds we hear, we must not only discriminate one sound from another, but we must be able to tell how sounds are similar. The ability to do this—perceptual constancy—is discussed by Patricia Kuhl, who uses the Visually Reinforced Infant Speech Discrimination method to assess perceptual constancy in infants. She also discusses the role of experience in the development of this skill.

In discussing these two papers, Lewis Leavitt of the Department of Pediatrics, Waisman Center at the University of Wisconsin called the VRISD technique a very promising one. However, he noted that one of its drawbacks is that it cannot be used during the first 4 or 5 months of life. Many have tried to modify the method for use with the very young infant, but it has been extremely difficult to do so. The VRISD technique also cannot be used beyond about 10 to 11 months of age, Leavitt said. The most promising and exciting aspect of this technique is its ability to tell us something about the individual infant. Earlier studies dealt only with group data. When it was reported that infants could discriminate *ba* from *ga* and *di* from *du,* that meant that a group of 10, 12, or 14 infants was able to do so because one or two of the sharpest babies pulled the group average up to a satisfactory level. What clinicians need to know, however, is not so much what the group can do, but what the individual infant can do in comparison with his peers. Can a particular infant discriminate between *ba* and *ga,* for example? The VRISD method may be a useful clinical tool and may make it possible to predict whether difficulties may occur in the child's later language development.

For the most part, speech is produced with the same musculoskeletal structures used for eating and breathing. It is a complex mechanism which is capable of producing a multitude of small-scale, rapid movements to produce the sound we know as speech. Infants develop the ability to make speech sounds like those produced by the adults around them, despite the fact that their speech mechanism is in an almost constant state of anatomical and physiological change.

Ronald Netsell describes speech as a motor control system—a system which governs the movements used in producing speech sounds and their combinations. He compares the adult mechanism with that of the developing infant. Netsell considers the babbling stage of speech sound production development to be of critical importance in diagnosing potentially abnormal speech production. He also suggests that a means of estimating what he calls the "Speech Motor Age" of the child would be a useful tool for describing an individual's speech motor control development.

Raymond Kent provides us with another perspective on the development of speech production skills. He emphasizes that it is the patterns of sound which we produce when we talk that are the link between speech perception and speech production. He also offers some insights into the nature and significance of babbling.

Leavitt commented that our current understanding of the neurobiology of humans is limited. For this reason, it should be kept in mind that the myelination data discussed by Netsell are based on the examination of a very small number of specimens and provide only a very general picture of developmental changes in the nervous system. Other research appears to demonstrate that the development of the nervous system is complex, but orderly, and affected by metabolism as well as environment. It has also been shown that the widely held view of the newborn baby as an organism with little or no central nervous system control of its actions and behaviors is quite false.

In spite of these cautions, Leavitt suggested that we pay attention to what is known about neuroanatomy and about the anatomy of the structures involved in speaking as we consider other aspects of the development of speech comprehension and production. He noted that the papers by Kent and Netsell are very important in helping us to take into account the limitations under which the infant and young child must operate in acquiring these skills. In terms of developmental anatomy, we do not have very good developmental landmarks, and we have no clear idea at present about the effects of environment, nutrition or differences in metabolism. We must therefore take our knowledge of anatomy into account as best we can; we must remain aware of new developments in the fields of anatomy and biology; and we should not regard existing data as fixed or unchangeable.

In the final paper in the section, D. Kimbrough Oller describes the infant as an active speech learner. He points out that the sounds babies make are largely related to adult speech sound patterns. Oller reflects a view of speech development which is dramatically different from those of many others. However, in light of the complicated non-verbal communication abilities of the infant which were described in Section I, it is possible to accept the idea that infant sound production is an intentional, organized, intelligent activity.

In discussing the papers in this section, Leavitt emphasized that it is important to try to integrate these studies of speech perception and speech production with what we know about cognitive development and the development of attachment and of social behavior. Leavitt and his colleagues have studied the vocalizations of 4-month-old infants. They observed that the infant's vocalization was a very important signal to the mother. She stopped talking, smiled, and then engaged in a whole series of other behaviors when the infant vocalized. The consequences of the infant's vocalization were complex, and contained a strong emotional component. Thus, infant vocal behavior is not only a basis for the later development of spoken language, but also has a powerful effect on the behavior of the caretaker.

In another series of studies, the Leavitt group asked how adults process infant signals. They found that the smiles and cries of infants stimulated strong physical responses in the mother. More interestingly, these responses were correlated with the mother's feelings about whether her own child was easy or difficult to care for. It was found that a mother who labeled her baby as "difficult" was less sensitive to changes in the signals produced by the infant. It has also been found that infants whose mothers were less sensitive to them performed at a significantly lower level on tests of cognitive development. This suggests that the interactions between mother and infant which later lead to the great complexities of human behavior and reactions found in family relationships may be related to communication and language development. It may therefore be of value to consider the quality and nature of mother-infant interaction as one of the determining factors in the development of language skills in the child.

Theories and Techniques of Infant Speech Perception Research

Rebecca E. Eilers, Ph.D. and William J. Gavin, Ph.D.

A number of theories have been proposed to explain the infant's ability to perceive speech. One theory is that speech perception skills are inborn or innate — the so-called phonetic innateness hypothesis. If these skills are innate, then we should be able to conclude a number of things about infant speech perception, based on what is known about adult speech perception.

Adults can discriminate between different classes of speech sounds, such as *b/d*. In addition, adults perceive consonants in a manner which is called "categorical." For example, an important acoustic difference between *pa* and *ba* is the time interval between the opening of the lips and the beginning of the vibration of the vocal cords for the vowel. This interval is called Voice Onset Time. Within certain limits, the longer the interval, the more likely the listener will be to hear *pa* rather than *ba*. Using electronically produced sounds, it is possible to make a tape recording of syllables in which the Voice Onset Time is increased in small steps from *ba* to *pa*. When English-speaking listeners are asked to label these syllables, they usually call them either *ba* or *pa*, but cannot "hear" the fine distinctions of the intermediate steps. Because this amounts to making each syllable fit either the *b* or *p* category, it is called "categorical perception". Consonants are perceived categorically but vowels are not. It is hypothesized that categorical perception is the result of the action of speech feature detectors in the brain, and that only speech, not noise or music, is perceived categorically.

In addition, if the infant is born with these perceptual abilities, it is logical to suppose that s/he does not need listening experience to process speech. A number of studies appeared to confirm some of these ideas, but recent work has thrown a different light on the innateness hypothesis, the role of experience, phonetic feature detectors, and categorical perception. This work suggests that speech perception does change and develop in infancy. The phonetic innateness idea is contradicted by data on difficult-to-discriminate contrasts. For example, infants have not demonstrated discrimination of *sa* from *za,* or *fa* from *tha*. These findings contradict the idea that every important speech sound category is discriminable by the infant.

WHAT ABOUT THE CLAIM THAT EXPERIENCE IN LISTENING TO LANGUAGE IS NOT IMPORTANT IN THE DEVELOPMENT OF SPEECH SOUND DISCRIMI-NATION ABILITY?   Several cross-language studies have shown that infants who have certain contrasts in their "native" language are able to discriminate them, while infants from language environments which do not include the contrast, do not discriminate them. This suggests that infants learn to discriminate the speech sounds of the language they hear around them, but are not born with the ability to discriminate the sounds of all languages.

WHAT IS THE ROLE OF FEATURE DETECTORS IN CATEGORICAL PERCEPTION?   Feature detectors are supposed to be located in a special area of the brain, the auditory reception area. They were thought to be activated automatically in the presence of speech sounds. These detectors were thought to be "tuned" so that perception would be better for some sounds and poorer for others. This helped to explain categorical perception. The feature detectors would make it easier for the listener to tell the difference between *b* and *p,* for example, but not between a number of *b*-like sounds. Recent research has raised questions about where in the auditory system these feature detectors could be located.

It has also been shown that categorical perception is not peculiar to the perception of speech, as was once thought. Musical sounds can be perceived categorically, by both adults and infants. Categorical perception of speech has also been shown to occur in animals. This aspect of speech perception, at least, does not appear to be unique to human beings.

It appears that speculation about innateness was premature because: infants have not been able to discriminate all speech contrasts; infants from different language environments show differences in discrimination performance; only some aspects of speech perception are categorical; phonetic feature detectors do not seem to underlie categorical perception; and speech sounds are not the only ones which are perceived categorically. Nevertheless, it is clear that *from an early age, infants are able to discriminate among a wide variety of speech sounds.* How this works is not well understood, but it seems logical to assume that the normal infant is at least in part constructed to decipher speech sounds.

In trying to understand infant speech perception, we must take into account factors such as the lack of physiological maturity of the infant's auditory system, the relative physical sound patterns of the various speech sounds, and the effects of environment and experience. Little is known about the structure and function of the developing auditory system, although from the structural point of view, much of the auditory system is virtually mature at birth. However, changes do occur during the first two years of life. Until the structure and development of the auditory system are more fully understood, it will be impossible to determine the relative effects of experience and maturation. In fact, there is the possibility that some aspects of physical maturation may be dependent on environmental factors.

THE RELATIVE SALIENCE OF ACOUSTIC STIMULI SHOULD ALSO BE TAKEN INTO ACCOUNT. Salience is the term Eilers and Gavin use to evaluate how easy or difficult it is for the listener to perceive differences between two or more sounds. For example, the acoustic events which cause us to hear stop consonants such as p/ t/ k don't last very long and are not as loud as the acoustic cues for vowels, which are longer in duration and relatively louder. The vowels would thus be said to be more acoustically salient than the stops. Similar judgments could be made concerning other types of acoustic cues. Of course, careful testing of these judgments is necessary.

Another important factor is *the nature of the infant's linguistic environment and experience.* How similar is a given contrast to any contrast which the infant has heard? How often has the baby heard such a contrast? It seems that when the infant hears a relatively difficult-to-discriminate contrast, s/he will find that unfamiliar contrasts which are similar to those s/he is familiar with will be easier to discriminate. But if a foreign contrast is highly acoustically salient, it would be easy to discriminate, regardless of experience.

In order for this description of infant speech perception to be useful, the notion of acoustic salience must be carefully defined in terms of experimental evidence. Likewise, the notion of similarity between acoustic events must be better understood, and the frequency of occurrence of various contrasts in a variety of languages must be determined. This framework seems to be a reasonable starting point for looking at the development of speech perception.

A number of procedures are presently available for studying infant speech perception: High Amplitude Sucking (HAS), Heart Rate (HR), and Visually Reinforced Infant Speech Discrimination (VRISD). Their important characteristics and some of their limitations are discussed below.

HIGH AMPLITUDE SUCKING (HAS) Infants are presented with a repeating speech stimulus, while the infant sucks on a nipple which is electronically connected so that the rate of sucking can be measured. The more the infant sucks, the more syllables s/he will hear. During the early part of the experiment, the number of high amplitude sucks typically increases to some point, remains steady, and then finally decreases. When the sucking rate decreases to a level set by the experimenter, the infant is said to have habituated to the stimulus. Then one of two events occurs. Half of the babies are presented with a new speech stimulus (the experimental group), and half are presented with the original stimulus (the control group). A significant increase in sucking in the experimental relative to the control group is accepted as evidence of discrimination. HAS procedures are applicable to infants 1 to 4 months of age. They typically can be used only to get group data, not information about individuals. Also, in a given group of infants, usually only a single pair of sounds can be tested. HAS has not been useful for looking at the relative ease or difficulty of discriminating various sounds, since the babies either suck or not, depending on which condition they are presented with.

HEART RATE (HR)   differs from HAS in that the infant does not control the presentation of the stimulus sound. Stimuli are presented in fixed patterns during which infant heart rate typically drops (decelerates). (Heart rate deceleration is an index of the orienting response in infants.) Each group of stimulus presentations is followed by a relatively long interval in which infant heart rate returns to normal. After several blocks of trials are presented, heart rate no longer drops and a new stimulus is introduced. If the orienting response recovers, that is, if renewed deceleration is found, it is concluded that the infant discriminated the new sound from the previous one. In practice, it is difficult to use this method beyond 5 to 6 months of age, because older infants are more active. HR procedures are most often applied to groups, but can be adapted for single subjects.

VISUALLY REINFORCED INFANT SPEECH DISCRIMI-NATION (VRISD)   involves the presentation of a repeating background stimulus which, at an appropriate point, is changed to some contrasting stimulus for a fixed interval, and then the original background stimulus resumes. During the presentation of the contrastive or test stimulus, a head turn by the infant toward the sound source (a loudspeaker) is reinforced by showing the baby a lighted, animated toy located on the loudspeaker. The measure of discrimination in VRISD depends on the comparison of turns to the test stimulus, versus turns during equivalent background intervals. VRISD has been successfully modified for testing categories of contrasts and for use in auditory sensitivity and speech discrimination testing.

This method is applicable to infants 6 to 18 months of age. It is useful across a broad age range and it can be used to assess a number of speech sound contrasts. Since the reward or reinforcement is not the speech signal itself (as in the HAS procedure), it is not necessary to assume that the speech signal itself is reinforcing or rewarding. Reinforcers, such as the lighted toy, can be chosen which maximize individual performance.

Development of statistical techniques to analyze data from VRISD studies has been prompted by the desire to answer the commonly asked question: Can infants discriminate a given contrast? While we do not have the tools to describe head-turn performance in VRISD for infants who *can* discriminate contrasts, we can describe the population of infants whose headturning performance is random. Having mathematically derived parameters for a population of infants whose headturning performance is random, we can then verify those parameters using computer simulation techniques.

In conclusion, we have presented evidence which suggests that the phonetic innateness theory of infant speech perception is not able to account for a variety of experimental results, including data from cross-linguistic infant studies, developmental studies, and studies concerning the relationship between categorical perception, speech detectors, and linguistic modes of processing. An alternative model was presented which takes into account innate abilities, and environmental effects. Finally, we have described the three most widely-used techniques for assessing infant speech perception abilities, and pointed out the strengths and weaknesses of these methods.

Perception of Auditory Categories by Infants

Patricia K. Kuhl, Ph.D.

Extensive study of speech sound discrimination in young infants, based largely on the high amplitude sucking technique, has shown that very young normal infants, 4 to 6 weeks of age, discriminate many of the acoustic cues underlying speech sound distinctions. They discriminate consonants that differ with respect to voicing (*p/b*) and place of articulation (*p/k*); they discriminate among fricative sounds (*th/sh*) and liquid sounds (*w/r/l*). Some of these contrasts have been tested not only at the beginning of a syllable, but also in the middle and at the end of syllables.

Infants also discriminate between vowels that are different (*i/u*). This is strong evidence that *the infant has sufficient auditory ability to discriminate the acoustic differences which typify many of the sound categories of English*. This is important, because if the infant could not perceive these differences, s/he would have an extremely difficult time learning language.

In addition to these abilities, however, *learning language would be aided by the perception of similarities between certain sounds*. To explain why this is important we have to take a look at the formation of auditory categories. The study of the categorization of speech sounds has usually focused on the perception of the boundaries between categories, for example the boundary between *b* and *p*. Under certain restricted testing conditions, a listener's ability to discriminate among sounds which vary only slightly is considerably better if the two sounds belong to different categories, such as *t/d*. Sounds which belong to the same category, but are slightly different, are not easily discriminated. It is this capacity which is generally called categorical perception. (See further explanation of this concept in the paper by Eilers. *Ed.*)

Another approach to studying speech perception is to describe the sound patterns that result in the perception of *similarities* for any group of sounds, all of which belong to the same phonetic category (different varieties of *t*, for example). Both of these approaches are related to the listener's tendency to form acoustic categories, that is, to give speech sound labels to various acoustic sound patterns.

Infants have been found to perceive electronically produced (computer generated) speech sounds in the same categorical manner as adults. This is extremely important to language development. If an infant can tell the difference between *p* and *b*, s/he has the basic skill necessary to distinguish between "pad" and "bad", for example. An important question is whether the human infant, at an early age, can discriminate *all* phonetic distinctions, even those not occurring in the language of his/her caretakers. If it were true that the infant could discriminate all phonetic distinctions found in all of the world's languages, then we could say that infants have an innate mechanism which enables them to perform this feat. In the course of development, however, the infant would seem to lose the ability to perceive contrasts not found in his/her "native" language, but would retain only the ability to distinguish among those that do occur in that language.

PERCEPTUAL CONSTANCY involves at least two processes. First, a listener must discover and focus on the important dimension that distinguishes the categories. In the second process a listener must ignore irrelevant sounds that are introduced when the phonetic context and the speaker are changed. For the infant to recognize that *di* and *du* are somehow similar, the vowels must be ignored. S/he must also ignore differences in the voices of different speakers since this is not important to identifying the *d* which is the sound common to the two syllables.

Recently, researchers have tried to find out whether infants are capable of recognizing the similarity among sounds that have the same phonetic label, when these sounds occur in different contexts (*pi/pu*), in different positions in a syllable (*pa, apa, ap*), or when they are spoken by different people. Several years ago, Kuhl and her colleagues began to test the infant's ability to form acoustic categories with a study of his/her perception of vowels.

Vowel perception is directly related to patterns of intensity (loudness) at particular points on the pitch scale from low to high. In natural speech, the vowel precedes or follows one or more consonants. This means that, in rapid speech, a pure vowel remaining steady for a detectible length of time is rarely spoken. In addition, a dramatic change in the acoustic pattern of a vowel occurs when that vowel is spoken by a male adult, a female adult, and a child. There is no simple, consistent relationship between the vowels as spoken by different talkers.

Kuhl and her colleagues wanted to know whether 4- to 16-week-old infants could detect a change in the vowel if an irrelevant factor was included as a kind of distraction. In one case, they wanted the babies to notice whether *i* or *u* had been said. They added pitch change as an irrelevant factor. Thus the baby had to ignore whether the pitch of the sound was high or low. In another case, they wanted the pitch to be noticed, and the particular vowel to be ignored. They found that the infants could tell the difference between the two vowels, regardless of pitch, and that they noticed the pitch change *only* when everything else was the same. The vowel seemed to capture the baby's attention more than the pitch change did. Using the head-turn technique for visual reinforcement with 6-month-olds, they also eventually found that the infants learned to recognize and discriminate two speech sounds, regardless of changes in pitch or speaker. Results such as these show that young normal infants are capable of recognizing important dimensions of sounds even when the task is fairly difficult. In order to do this, the infant must be able to develop rules for deciding what the essential characteristics of sound categories are. S/he must ignore very noticeable but unimportant dimensions of the sound such as pitch, talker and context, and must constantly monitor the signal and recall the rules of the "game". The fact that infants can do this should make coping with the world easier for them.

Despite much effort, research on infant auditory perception has somehow not yet been able to understand listening skills from the infant's point of view. The questions which need to be answered are: How does the infant use his/her auditory abilities to cope with living? To survive? These questions are not any better than those asked in the past, but they are different. Perhaps they will lead to the formation of a theory of the development of listening skills which takes into account how evolution has provided the infant with the means of communicating in the world.

SPEECH MOTOR CONTROL DEVELOPMENT

Ronald Netsell, Ph.D.

Speech as a motor control system undergoes a long period of development and may not be complete until early adolescence. It has several basic developmental requirements that have to do with the anatomy and physiology of the muscular, skeletal and nervous systems. It is paralled as a motor skill perhaps only by the skill of the unusual person who plays the piano entirely "by ear".

The physical act of speaking begins with commands from the central nervous system that control an elaborate complex of more than 100 muscles. When these muscles contract, they move various structures, which are shown in Figure 1. The movement of these bones, cartilages, and muscles produces a complex sound wave which we perceive as speech. Figure 1 also represents the speech mechanism as a set of ten functional components. A functional component is a structure, or set of structures, used to produce or interrupt the speech air stream. Information about movement of the physical structures, information about air flow, and information about the nature of the physical sounds produced gives us the most efficient way of describing the development of speech motor control.

The adult speech motor control system represents the end point of the developmental continuum. It serves as the model to which the developing system can be compared. In the adult, the greatest range of movement is performed by the lips, tongue and jaw, which move about 1 to 1.5 cm. These structures typically move at around 10 to 15 cm/sec, with maximums of about 25 cm/sec. The maximum rate of syllable production for the adult is around 6 per second. This maximum appears to be related to the rate at which the vocal cords or folds can be closed and opened across the outgoing air stream. In conversational speech, these in-and-out movements of the vocal folds are accomplished in about 75 to 100 msec.

An intriguing feature of the adult speech motor system is the "subconscious" manner with which speech movements are made. If normal adults hold rigid pieces between their teeth and say the vowel *i*, their tongues will assume almost the same position in the mouth as when speaking normally, and they will produce two *i* vowels which are nearly identical. They compensate for the pieces in the mouth without any awareness of repositioning of the tongue.

It would be interesting to learn when children develop "subconscious" control of their speech motor output. It has

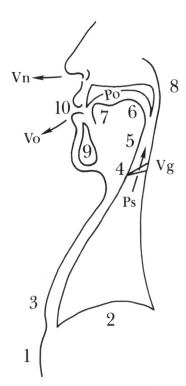

STRUCTURES

1-abdominal muscles
2-diaphragm
3-ribcage
4-larynx
5-tongue/pharynx
6-posterior tongue
7-anterior tongue
8-velopharynx
9-jaw
10-lips

AIR PRESSURES AND FLOWS

Ps -subglottal air pressure
Po -intraoral air pressure
Vg -glottal air flow
Vo -oral air flow
Vn-nasal air flow

FIGURE 1

been speculated that children place their emerging speech movements under a rather direct monitoring system. They use feedback as to muscular activity and the sounds produced, to help refine their control of the position and timing of speech movements. At some as yet undetermined point in development, these direct monitoring systems fade into the background, and the child no longer uses them. Whether or not children really use various kinds of feedback in a conscious or semi-conscious manner is not known. If they do, we have no idea as to when they begin to speak "unconsciously" or "automatically".

MATURATION OF THE NERVOUS SYSTEM AND MOTOR CONTROL The development of speech motor control seems to depend most upon maturation of the individual's particular nervous system. Critical periods seem to occur when certain neural, musculoskeletal, environmental and cognitive changes occur together in the individual. The points in time at which a particular number of these factors combines can result in developmental spurts that appear to be substantial leaps forward, if not placed in perspective with respect to sensorimotor and cognitive development.

The most noticeable motor act of the newborn for the listener is crying, which has its own developmental course. It is debatable whether the motor skills used in crying are used for speaking. The motor control patterns for sounds which infants make when they are not distressed are considerably closer to the motor controls used for speech. Speech-like sounds toward the end of the first 90 days of life are largely vowel-like, nasalized and of short duration. The newborn seems to be a rather simple sound generator by adult standards, but s/he may occasionally surprise him/herself and other listeners with "speech" simply by opening and closing his/her mouth while producing vocal sounds.

BABBLING This period of speech development may be the single most important one with respect to the eventual development of normal speech motor control. Delays or other abnormalities that appear or remain in this period would seem to have extremely serious consequences in terms of developing the basic motor patterns of speech production.

During this period, within the nervous system, connections are forming a network of loops, or circuits, that are important for fine motor control. Also of importance is the considerable myelination of the central auditory pathways. (Myelination is the growth of a fatty insulation, myelin, encasing the nerve fibers.) In beginning to speak while sitting up, the 3-month-old almost spontaneously assumes adult-like use of the rib cage and the abdomen. By 7 months, breathing patterns are essentially like those of the adult. The lower jaw grows rapidly down and forward, the larynx moves markedly downward, and the upper airway assumes more mature dimensions. The immature swallow pattern of the infant gives way to a more mature swallow in which the tongue is drawn back, rather than thrust forward, and there is more independence of lip and jaw movement. The appearance of front teeth may increase tongue retraction; lip, tongue and jaw movements become more independent in the early stages of chewing.

Against this background of maturation of the nervous system, growth of bone and muscle, and development of the face and mouth, is the ongoing emergence of more complicated and individually distinct movements of these structures for the motor control of speech. Two to four syllables appear in a single expiration, and the more typical shapes are consonant-vowel, vowel-consonant, and vowel-consonant-vowel. Somewhere between 3 and 9 months jaw independence from lower lip and tongue movements develops for most normal children, who have been said to produce such consonants as *r, s, z, th,* and *w*. A full range of vowels is also developed in this period. These sounds require shifts and shaping of the entire tongue body. In addition, the voiced/voiceless contrast (*b/p,* or *d/t,* for example) is established by 6 months. This suggests the beginnings of alternating action by the muscles which open and close the vocal folds. Finer variations in the pitch of the voice are also observed at this stage. Finally, the development of the ability to produce nasal versus non-nasal contrasts (*m/b, n/d*) indicates that at least gross contractions of the muscle which elevates the soft palate (levator palatini) are taking place.

TODDLER: 12 TO 24 MONTHS Most 12-month-olds are beginning to walk at about the time of their "first words". The practice of walking *or* talking seems sufficient to tie up all the available sensorimotor circuitry, because the toddler seldom, if ever, does both at the same time. This period is marked by considerable practice and refinement of speech motor skills, as well as acquisition of more and more complex speech movement patterns.

The emergence of "words" in this period coincides with the completion of myelination of the major neural pathways believed to be involved in speech motor control, and with a period of stabilization in musculoskeletal growth. By the end of this period, most normal children will have produced and practiced many times almost all of the single consonant and vowel combinations of their "native" language, including some consonant combinations. Speech movements are slower than those of adults, and the durations of the individual speech sounds are more variable than those of adults.

SPEECH MOTOR AGE   It may prove useful to develop a measure of the child's "Speech Motor Age". One way in which such an "age" might be represented would be to use overlapping time lines. The individual functional components of the speech motor system would be assigned a particular month-level, based upon the child's performance of selected speech motor acts. A complete Speech Motor Age chart would extend to perhaps 14 years, and the long-term goal would be to include speech motor acts that would make it possible to describe very small changes occurring throughout the speech development period. Such a chart would be based on a large body of perceptual, acoustic, and physiologic data taken from normally developing children. Given these data, it would be possible to assign a Speech Motor Age to a child. S/he may show a rather uniform delay in motor development across the component parts of the motor control system or may show differential problems in controlling the parts for speech. In either case, speech motor profiles might prove useful in implicating or ruling out neurological impairment of the speech motor output system.

Articulatory and Acoustic Perspectives on Speech Development

Raymond D. Kent, Ph.D.

Speech production is a highly precise and practiced motor skill, and its development involves changes in vocal tract anatomy, motor control of the articulators, and the use of the articulators and the larynx to produce audible, recognizable speech sounds. Speech is the use of the positions and movements of the articulators to produce an audible pattern of sound. These sound patterns are the link between speech production and speech perception.

During infancy and childhood, the vocal tract lengthens and changes its relative anatomical relationships. Because of these changes, it is likely that certain patterns of sound will be produced, and that the motor control of speech will have to be modified continuously during the course of development. Speech motor control has a complex course of development, from a simple organization of reflexes of the respiratory system, the larynx and the mouth, to a complex and flexible strategy of preprogramming which is conditioned by the language sounds the child hears. Preprogramming implies that movements are planned in advance and will eventually occur without the necessity of conscious monitoring by the speaker.

The vocal tract has evolved to have a short, broad oral cavity with a nearly right-angle bend where the mouth connects with the upper airway (pharynx); a tongue whose largest portion is toward the back of the mouth; a considerable separation between the epiglottis and the soft palate; a long pharyngeal cavity; and a larynx deeply recessed in the neck. Given such a vocal tract, exhaled air normally has access to the throat and mouth. This is distinctive of the human vocal tract, and underlies the human capability for speech production.

THE INFANT'S VOCAL TRACT differs from that of an adult in four major respects: the infant's tract is shorter; the pharynx is shorter and wider in relation to its length, principally because the larynx is high in the neck; the mouth is flatter than in the adult because of the absence of teeth; and the tongue more nearly fills the mouth. These differences in the anatomy of the mouth and pharynx between the infant and the adult are important when considering the relative potential for speech sound production of the two. Differences in vocal tract geometry mean that sounds resonate differently, and differences in the relative locations of the articulators mean that the muscles of the mouth and pharynx function differently. The anatomic differences between infant and adult imply that the motor activity of the articulators will be different.

The tongue of the infant is especially adapted to two motions, thrusting and rocking, both of which aid in grasping, suckling and swallowing. Tongue motion is restricted not only by the limited sensorimotor development of the organ, but also by the fact that the tongue almost fills the oral cavity. Generally, the earliest sounds of the infant are characterized by large and relatively un-differentiated tongue movements, as in the case of vowels (especially front vowels such as *i* and *u*) and the consonants *k* and *g*. More refined adjustments of tongue shape and position await the maturation of the intrinsic tongue muscles and a reshaping of the oral cavity to permit greater freedom of tongue movement.

Another example of changes in anatomy causing modification of motor control is the velopharyngeal mechanism, or the valve between the oral and nasal cavities. In normal adults, this valve or connection between the mouth and the nose can be closed by raising the soft palate. In fact, for swallowing, and for virtually all English speech sounds except the three consonants in the word "*meaning*", the valve is closed. However, the muscles which raise and stretch the soft palate in the adult actually stretch and *lower* it in the infant because of the location of these muscles with respect to the geometry of the head. With maturation, these muscles undergo a change of function. Given these anatomical characteristics, especially the approximation of the epiglottis and the soft palate, it is not surprising that nasalization frequently has been said to characterize infants' vocalizations. Because the presence or absence of nasalization is very important for the intelligibility of adult speech, developmental changes in the velopharyngeal region are highly significant.

The proximity of the epiglottis and the soft palate may have life-preserving value to the infant. With this arrangement, food can be swallowed on either side of the larynx/pharynx, thereby minimizing risk of choking. The separation of epiglottis and palate, and with it a transition from breathing through the nose instead of through the mouth, occurs between 4 and 6 months of life. It is interesting that babbling begins at about this same time. Perhaps disengagement of larynx and pharynx is an important anatomic condition for the appearance of this stage in communication development. Oller calls this period the expansion stage of phonetic development, one which is characterized by the production of adult-like vowels and diphthongs, and an increasing number of consonants. Before this time, most consonants appear to be formed in the back of the mouth (*k/g*) as opposed to the front where *p, b, m, t, d, n,* and many other consonants are produced by mature speakers.

Other changes in anatomy and physiology which occur at about this same time further prepare the child for speech acquisition. One of these changes is an increase in the duration of expiration. Lengthening expiration permits rapid inspiration at appropriate intervals. It also permits prolonged, primarily voiced expiration. Both of these are necessary for speech production.

Parallels between changes in vocalization during the first year of life and changes in the anatomy and physiology of the speech apparatus are summarized in Table 1. This table shows changes in anatomy and physiology corresponding to the major periods of speech sound development according to Oller. It appears that major changes in vocal behavior during the first year of life are related to significant remodeling of the anatomy of the vocal tract.

The so-called babbling stage of speech development is not easily defined, although it is usually said to occur somewhere between the 6th and 16th week of life. The child produces a variety of "sounds, repetitions, and adult-like intonation patterns." Babbling is a stage that precedes the emergence of a language-specific speech sound system, and provides considerable exercise of the speech organs.

Babbling does not seem to depend on normal hearing, for children who are deaf from birth apparently produce early babbling vocalizations similar to those of normal children. Therefore, babbling is not necessarily the same kind of integrated motor behavior as imitation and vocal exchanges between parent and child.

As far as the normal infant is concerned, it is usually assumed that babbling gives the child an awareness of his speech production capabilities. The association of auditory and motor events during babbling may also ready the child for the act of imitation.

BABBLING IS THE CHILD'S MEANS OF DISCOVERING HIS POTENTIAL FOR SPEECH PRODUCTION. From it

TABLE 1

Parallels between Stages of Phonetic Development (after Oller, in press) and Significant Anatomic-Physiologic Changes of Speech Apparatus.

Age of Infant	Phonetic Development	Related Anatomy and Physiology
0-1 month Phonation stage	Nasalized vowels	Nasal breathing and nasalized vocalization because of engagement of larynx and nasopharynx. Tongue has mostly back-and-forth motions and nearly fills the oral cavity.
2-3 months GOOing stage	Nasalized vowels plus g/k	Some change in shape of oral cavity and an increase in mobility of tongue.
4-6 months Expansion stage	Normal vowels	Increased separation of oral and nasal cavities, so that nonnasal vowels are readily produced.
	Raspberry (Labial)	The necessary air pressure in the mouth can be developed because of disengagement of the larynx from the nasopharynx.
	Squeal and Growl	Contrasts in vocal pitch are heightened perhaps because descent of larynx into neck makes the vocal folds more vulnerable to forces of supralaryngeal muscles.
	Yelling	Better coordination of respiratory system and larynx permits loud voice.
	Marginal babble	Alternation of full opening and closure of vocal tract is enhanced by larynx-nasopharynx disengagement.

s/he learns about the relationships between various articulatory shapes and the sounds they produce. S/he learns the relationship between one articulatory pattern and another, and between one sound and another. The infant also discovers how the articulators interact with one another. It has been suggested that a babbling infant might discover natural categories of sound production perhaps common to all languages. If so, then s/he may be predisposed to produce certain consonants and vowels. The task of learning speech would then be simplified for the infant, because crude speech sound categories could be developed through babbling.

Changes in infant sound production during the first year of life cannot be understood without careful consideration of anatomic development, maturation of neuromotor control, and the relationship between movements of the articulators and sounds produced. Just as the speech apparatus and its motor control are gradually reshaped by developmental processes, so is the acoustical signal which is generated by this apparatus. Various changes in anatomy and neuromotor control could lead to developmental discontinuities, or periods of relatively rapid and marked modification of function. The same processes may explain in part individual differences in development. Certainly, a variety of factors inevitably influence speech and language development. Anatomic remodeling, articulation-sound relationships, and neuromotor development are just a few of these factors, but their collective impact on early vocal behavior probably has been more often under-emphasized than over-emphasized.

Patterns of Infant Vocalization
D. Kimbrough Oller, Ph.D.

Are infant vocalizations a sign of developing intelligence and active learning, or are they simply instinctive, reflex acts? We will try to answer that question, although all of the pertinent information is not yet available.

INFANT VOCALIZATIONS ARE HIGHLY STRUCTURED AND IN MOST CASES ARE CLEARLY RELATED TO

ADULT SPEECH SOUND PATTERNS   Toward the end of the first year, infants produce syllabic babbling sounds, such as *baba, dede, ma,* which are very similar to the sounds used in children's first words. Babbling sounds resemble the most common speech sounds in the various languages of the world, with very few infant sounds being totally different from adult speech and language patterns. Each major sound type produced by infants, except for cries, grunts and the like, appear to represent the development of some crucial aspect of adult speech sound patterns. Thus it is possible to trace the relationship between infant vocalization and adult speech, starting from the first month of life.

How the infant uses his repertoire of sounds is also important. For example, infants commonly produce "coughs" in imitation of an adult. This imitation is a socially responsive act, in the same sense that mature speech is a social, responsive and communicative human activity. In general, as infants become capable of using speech-like sounds in more and more complex situations, they come closer to producing real speech, and their vocalizations demonstrate a higher level of intellectual development.

CAN IT BE SAID THAT INFANT SOUNDS ARE PURELY PASSIVE OR REFLEXIVE?   Two points seem to support this view: a large proportion of early sounds seem to be passive by-products of feeding and sucking. Even sounds which are not of this type seem to be produced in response to vocal stimulation. Such interpretations do not see the child as taking an active, intelligent approach to vocalization. However, many other kinds of evidence suggest that many infant sounds are not passive or reflexive. For example, when Oller and his colleagues studied the noises made by babies 1 to 4 months of age, they found that the babies adopted a particular pattern of vocalization, and repeated it for a while. This pattern was not related to the physical position of the baby (as some have suggested). Instead the baby seemed to repeat whatever sound type s/he was concentrating on at a given time. Why does the baby concentrate on particular sounds at particular times? It may be that infants vocalize according to certain rules, independent of environmental or physiological factors. Such a pattern does not seem passive.

A strict definition of a reflex says that the reflexive behavior can always be produced by a sufficiently strong and appropriate stimulus, and that the reflex response does not change much from one time to another. In asking whether or not some infant vocalizations are reflexes, we should look particularly at sounds other than pain cries, gags, and so forth, which are obviously reflexive. The real question is, are some of the more speech-like sounds reflexive during the first months of life, and if so, what is the stimulus that elicits them?

Our answer to this question, based only on casual observation, is that there is no environmental stimulus which always elicits speech-like sounds. Vocalizing, smiling and touching the baby are effective only a small part of the time. Furthermore, some individuals, often the mother or father, seem to be more effective in stimulating the infant to vocalize. This is not at all like reflexes, such as the knee-jerk, which occurs regardless of what the hammer looks like! Babies *do* seem to care who elicits vocalizations from them. Finally, even during the first 6 months of life, infant vocalization changes dramatically from month to month, and in some cases from day to day. Reflexes do not change in this way. It appears that infant speech-like vocalizations are not reflexive in a strict biological sense.

Departing, then, from the strict biological definition of a reflex, we might describe speech-like vocalizations in reflex terms by saying that the vocalizations can be elicited at least sometimes by the presentation of some definable stimulus like adult vocal sounds, facial expression or touch. However, the responsive vocalizations must be produced in a simple unthinking pattern to be called "reflexive". The research evidence does not show such simple patterns. For example, Bloom and her colleagues have shown that babies' vocalizations are a relatively high-level activity, similar to conversation. Infants seem to hesitate in order to determine whose turn it is to talk, or to figure out why the adult is doing something when the baby is vocalizing. Such cognitive activity is much more complicated than simple, reflexive behavior.

Even 1-month-olds have more than one speech-like vocal sound in their repertoire. We might ask why they choose particular sounds for particular situations. It has been widely stated that infant sounds are produced at random. However, recent research has contradicted this view. It seems that infants during the first 6 months are sensitive to vocal stimulation by adults. They are capable of responding vocally by either matching the adult sounds, or by producing sounds that systematically differ from the adult model, depending upon the circumstances. Such an ability is further evidence that infant vocalization is an intelligent activity, in which cognitive processes of sound recognition and vocal planning are involved.

There is also a communicative aspect to infant vocal behavior. In other words, the baby seems to use his sound-producing abilities to elicit particular behaviors from adults. For example, infants may learn to cry for attention. Whining also appears to be used to achieve some communicative or manipulative purpose beginning at a fairly young age, probably by 3 months. At 5 months, vocal game-playing with adults may occur. The child may produce a non-reflexive cough, for instance, expecting to elicit laughter or imitation from adults. It seems that infants vocalize selectively, in order to achieve complicated results in the world around them.

Infants also tend to produce repetitive sequences of vocalization during the vocal play or expansion stage of speech sound development. Is it possible that this repetitive behavior is a kind of practice? If so, it would seem that infants not only control the production of various sound types, but are *actively* learning to talk. There are two ways of describing the infant as an active, non-reflexive vocalizer. Both see the infant as an explorer, who investigates the production of various vocal sounds. The two views differ in that one assumes that the exploration is due to an interest in the vocal activity but not to an attempt to learn to talk. The other view says that the infant does have an overall strategy for learning to talk, and that vocalization practice is at least partly motivated by the desire to learn speech.

Presumably, by 2 or 3 months, the infant has an

understanding of "conversation". S/he may have come to understand that talking is a natural aspect of being human. In exploring vocal sounds, the infant may be partly spurred on by the desire to act like a human being talking. It is surely the case that at some point many children do become active language-learners. The question is: How soon? This may occur during the first 6 months of life in most normal infants. The 3- to 5-month-old understands and practices taking turns talking. S/he can and does vocalize and select matching sounds in response to adults. S/he communicates by making non-reflexive vocal requests; and s/he practices sound types selectively.

If the normal infant is engaged in the exploration of sounds, we would expect different tendencies in deaf infants. However, early evidence indicates that deaf infants generally produce sounds that are like those of hearing infants until about 6 months of age. Deaf and hearing infants may differ in the uses of vocalizations, the deaf being limited to utilitarian and face-to-face usage, while the hearing infants often vocalize purely for pleasure.

We have studied the vocalizations of a profoundly deaf baby, a victim of Waardenburg's syndrome, which is associated with hearing loss, but not with cognitive, speech-motor or other sensory impairments. Her vocalization from 8-18 months was clearly different from hearing babies'. Specifically, babbling in syllables was absent. Also, vocalization produced by deaf infants seems to have a high proportion of uncommon sound types for their age, although a full repertoire of normally expected pre-syllabic sounds does seem to occur, even as early as 8 months. This information on deaf infants suggests that during the first 6 months, babies do not have to hear their own sounds in order to develop some common pre-syllabic sounds. At the same time, the normal practical use of these sounds may be dependent on hearing.

Studies which compare the vocalizations of babies being raised in different language environments do not show that infants vocalize exactly alike regardless of language environment. But they do show a general similarity in vocalization across cultures. It seems that in exploring their vocal possibilities, infants have a tendency to use a relatively universal repertoire of sounds, at least up until the time that they start producing real words.

While it is possible that infants are simply exploring their sound-making capacities, and not "learning to talk," we believe that infants produce vocalizations in patterns that lend themselves to an interpretation as *speech* exploration and active *vocal communication* development. This interpretation is not the only reasonable explanation of infants' vocalization behavior during the first 6 months of life, but it is one option that spurs the imagination, and inspires yet deeper interest in the sounds of the human infant.

Chapter III
LANGUAGE AND THOUGHT AND THOUGHT AND LANGUAGE

(Discussant: Jerome Kagan, Ph.D.)

Jerome Kagan of Harvard University discussed the papers in this section and their relationship to three important questions, the first of which was: *Do language and thought develop in a related way, or independent of one another?* If language and thought develop in ways which are similar to the development of physical structures, Kagan said, then they probably develop independently, as do the tendons, cartilages and muscles of a particular joint.

Kagan's second quesiton was: *What is the relationship between a given developmental event, and the events which follow?* In biology, very often, a particular structure must be present in order for further growth and development to be possible. But the initial structure then disappears. "The caterpillar must exist first, but there is no part of the butterfly that can be identified in the caterpillar." Kagan suggested that there are probably many examples of this kind of relationship between the events or stages of psychological development as well. He pointed out that modern developmental psychology usually assumes that as the child matures, everything becomes more complex and therefore "better". Kagan believes, instead, that development is largely a process of simplification.

The third question emphasized by Kagan was: *Where do our constructs come from?* He suggested that researchers often begin with ideas about "sentences" or "words" and then try to find these constructs in the language behavior of children. He felt that this is not a particularly sensible way to study children. The application of abstract terms that are based on adult language to the speech and language performance of the child appeared to Kagan to be somewhat like using phylogenetic status to categorize a child's play with toy animals.

49

Kagan urged us to " ... observe the child and let him speak for himself." "The child ... is trying to communicate, to express excitement, to share interest, to get information, and he uses whatever means he can in order to do so." He summarized his view of the development of thought in relation to language as follows:

"During the opening years of life, I believe that the establishment of ... the ability to recognize the past and to retrieve the past, and the ability to make inferences and to operate in a linguistic mode, all develop in a relatively orderly sequence. These competencies follow the schedules of maturation of the central nervous system. The child's rate of development, which is genetically determined but also subject to environmental challenge, determines exactly when these competencies will appear. There may be a range of 3 to 6 months in their age of appearance, but the competencies are universal and will appear in all normal children."

The papers by Gerald Gratch, and by Kurt Fischer and Roberta Corrigan, offer two very different ways of describing the thinking processes of the young child. Each has its own implications for language development. For Gratch, the infant perceives the world differently than an older child. His/her mind is less orderly than Piaget suggested — it is more affected by environmental factors. For this reason, Gratch believes that thought and language interact and mutually influence one another. Fischer and Corrigan, on the other hand, propose a highly specific system for understanding the development of thought and language, based on skill theory. According to this theory, language development is a large set of partially overlapping, strictly defined skills, including listening, speaking, concept formation, and social interactions.

Kagan noted that Fischer and Corrigan describe some interesting new ideas which are not based on the theories of Piaget: that the child frequently is performing at his/her optimal level; that thought develops out of action; and that language and thought development can both be explained by skill theory. Kagan agreed that there are areas of activity at every age level in which the child *does not* operate at his/

her highest skill level. However, he pointed out that children appear to develop abstract ideas which do not come from actions, and that there is no necessary relation between the development of non-verbal thought and the development of speech.

The question of how children comprehend language messages is taken up by Robin Chapman, who finds that children seem, at first, to understand one word at a time. She also sees differences between what a child says, and what s/he understands. Somewhat surprisingly, she also reports that a child need not be at any particular level of cognitive development in order to understand certain language forms, and suggests that the role of environmental factors should be more carefully considered.

Lois Bloom and her colleagues argue that thought and language do not develop independently or simultaneously, nor in sequence, but are interdependent and overlapping. They also point out some of the pitfalls in using standardized assessment tools for evaluating the development of thought and subsequently determining the developmental relation between language and thought. They argue, instead, for observing the child's spontaneous behaviors in a naturalistic setting to infer progress in the development of thought.

The development of the ability to produce utterances which are organized according to grammatical rules is presented by David Ingram. He describes the early language of two young children, and points out that it is important to distinguish between non-rule-governed and rule-governed utterances in evaluating children's speech and language development. He also presents some evidence that cognitive development does not, in fact, affect grammatical development.

Arnold Capute and his colleagues describe the Language and Auditory Milestone Scale, a checklist designed for the use of pediatricians and allied health professionals in assessing early communication development. These authors emphasize that language development can be a valuable indicator of the presence or absence of a variety of disabilities, and a tool for predicting that a child is at risk to develop difficulties as s/he gets older.

Finally, Janet Hardy and Doris Welcher take a look at language development in several groups of handicapped children. Their paper not only offers an important clinical perspective, but eloquently describes some of the complexities of language as a neurologically based phenomenon. Of the papers included in the conference, those by Hardy and Welcher, and Capute and his colleagues, when considered against the background provided by the presentations of the other conference participants, are probably most directly of value to the clinical pediatric practitioner.

Some Thoughts on Cognitive Development and Language Development

Gerald Gratch, Ph.D.

Sometime during the second year of life, infants produce words relatively often, and provide relatively clear evidence of thought — they recall and they pretend. Before that time, they are highly dependent upon their caretakers, and signs of talk and thought are not obvious. One general way of trying to organize these observations has been to make a distinction between animal and human nature. Animals are not human because they don't talk and think, and infants are not fully human or intelligent or capable of sentiment, or having deep attachments to their caretakers, before they think and talk.

Our focus is on a particular version of the animal-human idea. It presumes that before you can talk about something meaningfully, you must have an idea of it. It is also assumed that we can determine the existence of ideas by studying how the infant acts with respect to objects which are not present. Is "out of sight, out of mind" or can the infant image the object and search for it? According to this point of view, the infant first perceives definite objects, and then becomes "human" by having an idea of objects when they are absent. During this time, the infant also learns to label these objects and eventually uses these labels to think about the objects, even when the objects are absent. Usually, labeling is thought to come about through a process of point-and-name.

This approach is not unreasonable, yet the point-and-name game rests on the assumption that the infant and the adults are both talking about the same thing. However, recent research on the nature and development of language has dramatized the fact that words and sentences do not refer to events in an unequivocal way. Many have felt that they could understand how infants come to think and talk by combining a practical view of linguistic meaning with Piaget's ideas about the achievement of the sensorimotor infant. Both sets of ideas lead to attempts to discover which of many possible events the child has in mind when he focuses on a common situation with an adult. But the two sets of ideas diverge when we consider Piaget's view of the structure of the child's mind and how it develops.

The particular aspect of Piaget's idea about the development of thoughtfulness in infancy that fits the line of reasoning outlined above, is his description of the development of the object concept, the idea of object permanence. Piaget's work is based on the key notion that we can infer the presence or absence of ideas from how infants deal with non-present objects. He emphasized that hidden object problems may be solved in thoughtless as well as thoughtful ways and focused on describing *what* aspects of the situation the infant had in mind, not on *whether* the infant could remember the missing object. In this respect, Piaget was influenced by the Gestalt approach to problem-solving, which emphasized that objects exist in contexts, and that how one sees the relation between the object and its background determines the meaning of the figure. The fundamental issue in perception and thought was organization, the organization of the mind and of the world, and how they come together.

Piaget basically described the development of the object concept as occurring in three steps. In the first, "out of sight is out of mind". Young infants might continue to focus on hidden objects, but Piaget argued that such orientations were the continuation of actions which started when the object was in view.

The second step illustrates Piaget's emphasis on *what* rather than *whether*. In this step, the infant is able to find the hidden object in a way that is not simply continuing an ongoing action. To get the toy, the infant must stop reaching, must keep his "eye" on the goal, and also focus on whatever it is that is concealing the object. By 8 or 9 months, infants do this in a relatively skilled way, and it is tempting to conclude that the infant's search is guided by an "image" of the missing toy. Piaget reasoned differently. In plain view of the infant, he hid the object in a second well-marked place. The infant watched, and then went directly to the first place. Piaget concluded that infants in this phase of development still see objects in space in terms of their egocentric action schemes, and do not represent missing objects.

In the third step, the infant shows true intelligence, and is able to represent mentally the missing object, and its possible locations. The infant can then solve invisible displacement problems, ones where the infant can only see that the object is in one of several possible places and must figure out the correct one.

What is fascinating about Piaget as an observer is how he can surprise us. He leads us to believe that the child understands the focal event, the mutual topic, just as we do. But a seemingly unimportant change in what we do, such as spreading out one row of pennies and not the other, or hiding an object in a second place, is treated as very important by the child.

There are various ways to describe what infants have in mind when they make an "error." One is in terms of the rule of the game, namely that the toy is in the place where it disappeared. In playing the game with some infants, we found that it took a couple of months for an infant to figure out this rule. Initially, the infants would not try to correct themselves. Later, they did, and still later they would search correctly, but only after looking at or touching the first hiding place. The infants appeared to learn about each hiding place separately. When they developed the capacity to search only where the toy was hidden, introduction of yet another hiding place confused them again.

Another approach is to focus on the characteristics of the hiding place. Making the covers and their backgrounds more distinctive decreases the likelihood of error.

Varying where the hiding places are situated in relation to
the infant also affects the error. When the desired object is
at the midline and is attached to a string or rests on a
support, then the infant is more likely to use an available
tool to get at an object than when it is off to one side. But
the infant is also likely to use a "tool" located at the
midline, even when it is clearly not attached to the object
which the infant is attempting to get. These examples
bring out two points. One is the importance of what the
infant is perceiving. The other is that we can structure a
situation so that it will be easier for the infant to act
appropriately, but it is not at all clear that the infant sees
the situation in the same way we do.

In the third step, Piaget's stage 6, the infant frees
himself from the sensorimotor stream, and a coherent
organization of mental schemes permits the infant to
distinguish self from object, locate objects in a system of
possible places, recall events and plan for non-present
events. Piaget now attributes concepts to the infant, and
believes he is intelligent. It is this view of the infant as
possessing a definite mind in the second year of life that
has attracted many investigators who were trying to develop an account of the development of language as a
symbolic system. But how clear a mind is it?

A number of years ago Gratch was trying to study how
children come to understand the structure of that common game, sometimes called, "Guess which hand I'm
hiding the marble in?" With 18- to 24-month-olds, he
started by hiding the marble and holding his hands in
front of him. When he shifted his hands behind his back,
even turning around so they could see his hands, they
became disoriented. The babies had little understanding
of this rather simple change in the spatial layout of the
game. Even more to the point was his experience with
another child, age 2 years. They played with the hiding
being done hands-in-front. For about 15 trials Gratch
alternated the hand containing the marble, and the child
quickly began to guess successfully each time. Finally, he
did not alternate. The boy opened the empty hand, was
dismayed, and then began to hunt for the marble in and
around the couch they were sitting on, ignoring the other

hand entirely. He was obviously not engaged in a systematic analysis of the display. In fact, his search was similar to the behavior of the 9-month-olds described above.

Gratch also tried a simple version of the "shell game". The examiner places the toy under one of two covers and then, in full view of the infant, exchanges the places of the covers. Many of the 15-month-olds he tested did not solve this simple version of the "invisible displacement" problem.

These observations illustrate that there are many ways in which the older infant fails to keep on top of where the covered object is, even though he seems to have a relatively clear idea about the relation of the object to the cover.

While there is much merit in Piaget's attempts to find a kind of developmental order that would underlie a connection between the many variations in task and infant response, my quarrel is with how he conceptualizes the process. In Piaget's view, the newborn begins with small segmental schemes that order sensations in a small way, which finally lead to an organization of the schemes — a logic of action which permits symbolic action. Piaget's primary focus was on identifying the schemes that ordered the sensory array, rather than in seeking order *in* the sensory array. His aim was to capture the mental processes which order the various lessons that caretakers and nature offer to, and impose upon, the child. But, he sees too much internal order in the infant, and he gives the environment too secondary a role in the development of thoughtful action and talk.

What are the alternatives? The answer may lie in the ideas of Vygotsky. He saw thought and language as a process of coming together, thought from the inside out, language from the outside in. The interaction of culture and individual was seen as a transactional process, and the results of this process could not be analyzed solely with respect to the individual, or the environment. Vygotsky traced a process of outer to inner speech, wherein the latter was an attempt to express the idea that we think with words and images, taking into account the audience we want to share our ideas with. When we talk with strangers, we must be articulate if we are to be understood. With friends, we can be less explicit, and Vygotsky saw thought as a very inexplicit conversation with a very familiar person, ourself. With such a view, Vygotsky tried to show how thought shifts from "autism" to self-control through the internalization of the control of others. For Vygotsky, the situational context was central to determining communication both in the moment and in the course of development.

Piaget considered the environment only superficially and emphasized that it exists in the mind, only insofar as it is assimilated into the organism. His aim was to capture the activity of reasoning in terms of a mind that is structured logically, and to chart its development from a series of lesser logical structures.

In learning language, the words, ideas and natural events that the child ill-understands, are reduced by the child to his own terms and lead him to act and know in those terms. When we "put on airs" in adolescence and childhood, there is a sense in which we do what we don't know, but there is also a sense in which such behavior is the necessary step towards becoming what we have the capacity to be. It's a kind of trial and error process that operates all through life. In learning language, the child doesn't know what s/he is trying to learn, and situations are not so clear that either the parent or the theorist can describe them in unambiguous terms.

Thus there is a parallel between what goes on in learning "object permanence" and in learning how to talk. In language games, many have noticed how the parent tries to highlight what s/he says and what it refers to. So, too, in hiding games, the examiner can facilitate the child's search for hidden objects by making certain features and relations more obvious. But in neither case does the child learn a large and unambiguous lesson. We must allow for the child to be an actor who at times reflects on what he and others do, and tries to figure out what is happening. In both infancy and adulthood, thought and talk may help us to "objectify" our experience, but there is less logical order in such activity and its development than Piaget and some linguists seem to suggest.

A Skill Approach to Language Development

Kurt W. Fischer, Ph.D., and Roberta Corrigan, Ph.D.

According to most modern approaches to language development, the child develops very general rules for learning language. By the age of 2 years, children are assumed to use rules involving abstract categories like nouns and verbs. The Piagetian approach to cognitive development makes the same general assumption: that children develop very broad schemes, such as object permanence, causality and means-end relations. Developments in cognition are assumed to be prerequisites for language development.

During the past ten years a number of people have challenged this assumption of the general nature of language and cognitive development, and have begun to describe these aspects of child development in much more specific terms. Early language rules are described as fairly specific, limited behaviors, which the child gradually builds into generalized rules of language. Likewise in cognitive development, schemes or skills are assumed to be relatively specific to a given situation.

Skill theory describes language as a large set of partially overlapping skills. Thought, in general, is not something that must precede language in general, nor vice versa. A skill is an organized ability that is composed of one or more components under the control of an individual. The components can be actions, representations, or abstractions. For example, a 3-month-old may be able to grasp her rattle. By 7 months, she has combined the grasping skill with a listening skill to form a single, new, and more complex skill—grasping the rattle to hear it.

A skill is jointly determined by the person's actions and the environment. Skills are therefore relatively specific. This differs markedly from Piaget's approach, which says that the *child* is at a particular developmental stage. Skill theory says that a *skill* is at a particular level. Each child has many different skills at a variety of levels, at any given time. Strictly speaking, there is no such thing as a developmental "stage".

Skill theory explains major shifts in development

through the construct of *optimal level*. Optimal level is the most developmentally advanced performance that a child shows across a wide range of skills. The skills that s/he practices frequently will usually be at this highest level, but other skills will not. Optimal level increases with age, but not at a constant rate. There are periods of relatively faster or slower change. These changes in rate mean that children at a given level should be able to master more complex steps within their level, but not even the simplest step at the next level. Language skills are at least as good a measure of optimal level as performance on Piagetian tasks.

In skill theory, there are ten successive optimal levels through which a person develops from birth to adulthood. The levels specify skills of gradually increasing complexity, with a skill at one level built directly upon skills from the preceding level. The progression of skills shows a repetetive cycle with the structures of levels 1 to 4 parelleling those of levels 4 to 7 and 7 to 10 as shown on Table 2. Each cycle is called a "tier" and specifies skills of a different type: sensorimotor, representational, or abstract. A "system" is the ability to control relationships between at least two different aspects of each of two components. At the highest level within each tier, the child can coordinate two or more systems into a single, new skill. This allows him/her to use one system to cognitively control another system, and generates the new type of skill for the next tier. Thus, the fourth level of one tier is also the first level of the next tier. This scheme of development is diagrammed in Table 2.

Skill theory has been used to predict a number of developmental sequences and other developmental phenomena, involving self-recognition, classification, social skills, object permanence, agent use, social role-playing, and spontaneous play. Table 3 shows a detailed social-cognitive sequence of the development of agent use and social roles. Most of the steps in this sequence have been verified experimentally by Watson and Fischer.

According to skill theory, the number of steps within a level can be so numerous and involve such small differences that the scale is essentially continuous. The num-

TABLE 2

The Ten Developmental Levels Described by Skill Theory			
Tier		*Level*	*Structure*
Sensorimotor	1	1	Single Sensorimotor Action
	2	2	Sensorimotor Mapping
	3	3	Sensorimotor System
Representational	1 |4|	4	System of Sensorimotor Systems = Single Representation
	2	5	Representational Mapping
	3	6	Representational System
Abstract	1 |4|	7	System of Representational Systems = Single Abstraction
	2	8	Abstract Mapping
	3	9	Abstract System
	4	10	System of Abstract Systems

ber of "steps" that a child actually shows, however, is a function of the child's environment. By testing the child on a finely graded sequence, the testing procedure itself actually produces a finely graded, continuous scale of development.

It is commonly assumed in research on language development and cognitive development that most children show the same sequence of development in a given domain. But given the effects of different environments, individual children are not as similar as they seem to be. Skill theory starts with the assumption that environmental factors must be taken into account from the very beginning. Another troublesome problem in the study of development is that *behavior is ambiguous.* Children may use very different strategies to produce behaviors which, on the surface, look identical. By determining what skills are required to perform a task, and by reducing the number of approaches that the child can use to perform each task, we will get a clearer idea of what the child's behavior means. The test task is a major determinant of both the age at which a skill is first detected, and the sequence in which it develops with respect to other skills. This is especially important with respect to the assessment of language development. Some have tried to avoid diffi-

TABLE 3

A Developmental Sequence of Agent Use and Social Roles in Pretend Play

Step	Cognitive Level	Type of Skill	Example of Behavior
1		Self as Agent	Child pretends to go to sleep.
2		Passive Other Agent	Child pretends to put doll to sleep.
3		Passive Substitute Agent	Child pretends to put a toy block to sleep.
4	4: Single Representations	Active Other Agent	Child pretends that a doll goes to sleep, acting on its own.
5		Active Substitute Agent	Child pretends that a toy block goes to sleep, acting on its own.
6		Behavioral Role	Child makes a doll carry out several actions appropriate for a doctor, like taking a patient's temperature and putting the patient in bed.
7		Shifting Behavioral Roles	Child makes one doll carry out several actions appropriate for a patient, like saying it is sick and going to bed, and then makes a second doll carry out several doctor actions.
8	5: Representational Mappings	Social Role	Child makes a patient doll and a doctor doll interact, showing several appropriate behaviors.
9		Shifting Social Roles with One Common Agent	Child makes two dolls interact as doctor and patient and then makes the patient doll interact with a nurse doll.
10		Social Role with Three Agents	Child makes three dolls interact as doctor, patient, and nurse.
11		Shifting Social Roles for the Same Agents	Child makes two dolls interact as doctor-patient and then makes them interact as father-daughter.
12	6: Representational Systems	Social-Role Intersection	Child makes two dolls interact simultaneously as doctor-patient and father-daughter.
13		Shifting Social-Role Intersections with One Common Agent	Child makes two dolls interact simultaneously as doctor-patient and father-daughter and then makes the man-doll interact with another doll as doctor-mother of patient and husband-wife.
14		Social-Role Intersection with Three Agents	Child makes three dolls interact simultaneously as doctor-patient-mother of patient and father-daughter-wife.

Note: This sequence is based on research reported in Watson (1977) and Watson & Fischer (1977, 1979).

culties associated with language assessment testing by analyzing spontaneous language produced by the child. This does not solve the problem posed by the ambiguity of behavior. In fact, it often increases it.

When the developmental relationship between two distinct skills is being investigated, the most straightforward approach is to measure the two skills with tasks that are as nearly identical as possible. Research relating language and cognitive abilities has almost always used dissimilar tasks, however. It is not surprising, therefore, that studies designed to assess the same two abilities, for example, object permanence and single-word use, have produced contradictory results. The Piagetian literature on the development of cognition demonstrates repeatedly that most children share sequences of development, even across very different social groups. The language development literature, on the other hand, shows a high frequency of individual differences in development. This discrepancy between what is said about language development and what is said about cognitive development, apparently has come about because different methods have been used to study the development of the two abilities.

LANGUAGE LEVELS   For any skill, including language, it is important to realize that there is no one true developmental sequence that all children will show. Rather, the language that a child produces will be determined largely by his individual language environment, and by the method used to evaluate his/her language skills. Language involves many different sets of skills, including vocalization, articulation, hearing, concepts to be talked about, social interactions, and much more.

Early speech is not representational, according to skill theory. That is, the early words and phrases produced by a child probably do not refer to objects and actions in the way that adult language does. For adults, the word is a symbol for the object. For the young infant, a word is simply the result of certain coordinated sensorimotor actions, such as vocalization and hearing. Early words do not "mean" anything to the child. Eventually, the child is able to control variations in his actions, because s/he has developed the ability to control more than one action at a time. This enables the child to imitate new sounds, including simple words and even two-word utterances.

Language ultimately requires social skills. The child must be able to figure out what someone else means, and communicate his/her own intentions. However, the skills

involved in producing language may be developed somewhat independently of the skills involved in social interaction, and communication can certainly occur without
language. Some believe that skills for non-verbal communication develop during infancy, and are used later
when communication involving language develops.
Comprehension seems to involve communication, but
the degree to which this aspect of communication is verbal
is not clear. For example, Chapman points out that the 1-
year-old may appear to understand complete sentences,
but s/he really does not understand them. The child is
simply "doing what s/he usually does in the situation." S/he
pays attention to the individual object that is named, but
acts on that object not according to what s/he may be asked
to do with it, but according to what s/he normally does
with that object in a given context. In other words s/he
simply coordinates hearing a single word with a familiar
action.

*SKILLS FOR LANGUAGE COMPREHENSION AND PRO-
DUCTION*   seem to be only partly overlapping, but there
should actually be little difference between the kinds of
utterances that are understood by the child and those that
s/he produces, since they both involve control of the same
types of words and the same relationships among words.
According to skill theory, both single words and some
limited two-word utterances can be produced and understood using fairly simple sensorimotor skills. For example,
by experimenting with variation on his vocalizations, the
child can discover how to produce a sound equivalent to
what s/he has just heard. This word can then be gradually
dissociated from the process of imitation and become
attached to other sensorimotor actions of the child. Corrigan reported an example where a mother said "light"
every time her infant pulled a cord to turn on a light. After
a while the baby imitated the mother's utterance, and
eventually, the word became associated with the skill of
pulling the cord. Skills like this are sensorimotor. They
involve the coordination of a number of aspects of several
actions into a single skill (a system), but they do not involve
coordination of more than one system into a single skill.

At a later stage, the child coordinates two or more separate systems into an integrated, higher-level unit, so that while s/he is actually carrying out one system, s/he can be thinking about another one. By coordinating two sensorimotor systems, the child can learn a large number of single words. With one system s/he learns to say the word; with the other, s/he carries out the actions and perceptions to which the word refers. This provides him/her with the meaning of the word. The child can then learn new words easily, and there is a spurt in vocabulary growth.

After reaching the skill level which results in a rapid growth of single-word vocabulary, the child builds more complex language skills for at least a year. Then s/he moves beyond the ability to represent single actions or objects with single words, and develops more complicated language skills. S/he then begins to be able to construct skills for saying more complex sentences, for producing more complex sounds, and for understanding more complicated messages. S/he can monitor his/her own production better, take the perspective of others more successfully, and eventually write prose or give speeches.

Language Comprehension and Cognitive Development

Robin S. Chapman, Ph.D.

In our studies of children in the second year of life, we asked all three questions posed by Kagan:

1. How do children's skills in understanding language change?

2. What is the relation of the development of thought to changes in language comprehension?

3. When we look at children's compliance with requests to attend and act in their natural interactions with their mothers, what can we learn about comprehension development?

Our work on these three questions is summarized under the headings of *Testing for Changes in Language Comprehension; Cognitive Prerequisites to Comprehension;* and *Comprehension in the Natural Context.*

*TESTING FOR CHANGES IN LANGUAGE COM-
PREHENSION* We are interested in determining how
many of the words in a sentence children really need to
understand before acting appropriately in response to a
message; how they perform on communication games like
"peek-a-boo" and "patticake"; and how they understand
references to present versus absent objects. It is important
to remember that the child may respond to cues other
than, or in addition to, the sentence s/he hears. Possible
strategies used by young children are outlined in Table 4.

TABLE 4

Summary of Nonlinguistic Response Strategies and Comprehension Strategies Proposed for Children 8 to 24
Months (Adapted from Chapman, 1978)

Approximate Piagetian Stage and Age Range	*Possible Responses*
SENSORIMOTOR STAGE IV (8-12 months) Context-Determined Responses	1. Look at objects that mother looks at 2. Act on objects that you notice 3. Imitate ongoing action
SENSORIMOTOR STAGE V (12-18 months) Context-Determined Responses With Comprehension of Object Name	1. Attend to object mentioned 2. Give evidence of notice 3. Do what you usually do in the situation

SENSORIMOTOR STAGE VI (18-24 months) Word Comprehension; Context Determines Sentence Meaning	1. Locate the objects mentioned and give evidence of notice or
	2. Do what you usually do
	  a. Objects into containers
	  b. Conventional use
	3. Act on the objects in the way mentioned
	  a. Child as agent
	  b. Choose handier object as instrument

An examiner must be sure that the child is not using one of the simpler strategies before assuming that the child's performance is related to his/her understanding of the vocabulary or grammar of the instructions.

For example, the examiner must not gesture or look at the objects mentioned in an instruction. Requests for actions that are usually performed with the object the child is playing with must be excluded as evidence for comprehension; and the child's ability to assign an agent role to a noun in an utterance must be tested without using the child as the agent (see examples in Table 5).

The eight comprehension items that we have tested are summarized in Table 5. The examiner first attempted to establish evidence of comprehension at least twice on the one-word items (1 - 4). If the infant understood these single words, then the examiner went on to the multi-word items (5 - 8). First, we got the child's attention, usually by calling his/her name. When eye contact was established, the request was presented in forms such as "where's X?" "lookit X" "wanna X?" "can you X?" At 10 to 12 months the children understood the names of people better than the names of objects. All the children understood at least their own name and "mama." Comprehension seemed to be restricted to words which referred to objects and people who were present. Not until 18 months did half the children begin to pass the items which referred to absent persons or objects. Verbs began to be understood, as indicated by children's actions, between 13 and 16 months.

ONE WORD AT A TIME   Infants 10 to 16 months old seem to be able to process only one word at a time. This may mean that the child's ability to understand what the mother says is best for single-word utterances, or for the last word in the mother's sentence, since this word would be easiest for the child to remember. Comprehension of at least two words was shown by 17-month-olds for items like *Mama's shoe;* by 18-month-olds for items like *Kiss the shoe;* and by 19-to 20-month-olds for sentences such as *Horsey eat.* Children bring their own interpretations to what the speaker means by the words. *Mama's shoe* may be responded to by handing mother a shoe as well as by

TABLE 5
Comprehension Test Items
(adapted from Miller, Chapman, Branston, and Reichle, 1980)

Item and Examples	Passing Response	Age at which 50% pass
1. PERSON NAME *Where's* (child name)? *Where's Mama? Where's* (X)?	Child indicates himself or mother or other known present person in response to question.	Under 10 mo.
2. OBJECT NAME *Where's* (X)? *Go get* (X). *Give me* (X). X = words supplied by mother; *shoe, hat, diaper, stuffed animal* (brought from home), *ball, book, pencil, cup, bottle, table* or *chair*	Child looks at, gets, shows, or gives the appropriate object among several present in visual field.	12 mo.
3. ABSENT PERSON OR OBJECT Item passed from #1 or #2	Child searches for a person or object when it is out of view.	18-20 mo.
4. ACTION VERB (V) (*it*) *Wanna* (V) (*it*)? *Can you* (V) (*it*)? V = verbs supplied by mother; *kiss, tickle, pat, hug, smell, blow, eat, throw, open, close, drink,* and *bang* or *hit*	Child complies, he may already be attending to the object. If so, the requested action cannot be one conventionally associated with the object.	13-16 mo.

TABLE 5 *(cont.)*

Item and Examples	Passing Response	Age at which 50% pass
5. POSSESSOR— POSSESSION a. *Where's mama's shoe?* *Where's Joshua's shoe?* b. *Where's Mama's chair?* *Where's Joshua's chair?* Person and object names from those passed in #1 and #2.	Child appropriately locates the correct person's object both times, among present people and objects.	17-18 mo.
6. ACTION— OBJECT *Kiss the shoe.* *Can you hug the ball?* *Wanna pat the book?* Verbs and objects are those passed in #2 and #4	Child complies for the appropriate object among several present. He cannot already be attending to the object; action should not be conventionally associated with object.	18-19 mo.
7. AGENT (other than child)— ACTION *Horsey eat.* *Make the doggie kiss.* *Wanna make the horsey eat?* Verbs and objects are those passed in #2 and #4	Child selects toy among several present and demonstrates action with the toy serving as agent. Action should not be probable for the toy.	19-20 mo.

TABLE 5 *(cont.)*

Item and Examples	Passing Response	Age at which 50% pass
8. AGENT (other than child)— ACTION— OBJECT *Horsey kiss the ball. Can doggie eat the diaper?* Verbs and objects are those passed in #2 and #4.	Child selects appropriate toy and object among those present and demonstrates appropriately. Action not probable for agent or object.	Over 21 mo.

looking at her shoe. There seems to be a difference between what the child is likely to say at this age, and what s/he is likely to understand as the intended message. For the child, what is worth talking about is what is new; what the child can understand is what is familiar, or "old."

During the second year of life, the child appears to have very limited and simple skills in language comprehension. S/he understands words rather than sentences. At 10 months s/he understands one word at a time, at 18 months, two words at a time. These characteristics of the infant's language *comprehension* may help to explain why children start talking by using one word at a time. The kind and simplicity of grammatical patterns used by the mother during the second year of life may be irrelevant to the child's comprehension and production development, since his/her limited comprehension skills would mean that s/he would only grasp one or two words, regardless of what the mother said.

COGNITIVE PREREQUISITES TO COMPREHENSION? To answer the question of whether children must have certain cognitive or mental abilities in order to understand language, we compared the results on our comprehension tasks with results on cognitive tests drawn from the Uzgiris and Hunt Ordinal Scales of Psychological

Development and other scales that were developed to evaluate sensorimotor development following the ideas of the Swiss psychologist, Jean Piaget. It is usually said that a child must have reached a certain level on these tests before being able to use and understand language forms. We did not find this to be so. For example, some children who did not seem to have a concept of the permanence of objects, nevertheless passed the comprehension items involving absent people and objects, and action verbs. These items are usually said to depend on the earlier development of object permanence.

A more general way of looking at the relationship between cognition and comprehension is to estimate the child's general cognitive level, rather than his/her performance on particular tasks. Having done this, we can evaluate whether this estimate is a better predictor of the child's comprehension abilities than is the child's chronological age. We have found that both age and cognitive level plus his/her experience predict comprehension; but age is a better means of predicting the child's comprehension performance than is cognitive level alone. This is because age is indicative not only of cognitive level, but of maturational level and amount of experience.

In some children, the mentally retarded for example, age is not a good predictor of skills. Would cognitive level predict comprehension skills in these children? In a clinical study of 26 developmentally delayed children, chronological age was indicative of the experiences of the child, but not of cognitive level. For this group, cognitive measures were better predictors of the upper limits of language functioning. We conclude that general cognitive level, as determined by a child's performance on a variety of sensorimotor tasks, can be a useful guide to the language comprehension abilities of developmentally disabled children. In establishing expectations for normal children, however, age seems to be the best indicator of comprehension ability.

COMPREHENSION IN THE NATURAL CONTEXT All the questions posed so far have been about children's understanding of word and sentence cues. Kagan is right to remind us, however, to look at the child's performance in natural contexts; to ask what cues the child *ordinarily* uses. Our experimental studies have shown that at best, one or two words out of a sentence might play a role in determining one- to two-year-olds' responses. Yet mothers of these children report that they understand everything. Are the mothers right? What additional cues to comprehension are present in the natural context? To answer these questions, we have looked at children's responses to mothers' requests to attend to objects and act on them in free play.

In studying the gestures and cues which mothers provide to the infant, we have found that gestures accompany almost all requests by mothers to attend to an object. Mothers almost always choose a nearby object to talk about; they point out objects and show how they can act, often by moving them in some way. These behaviors by the mothers seem to explain why they are almost always successful in getting the children to attend to objects. The child will usually turn toward the mother when she speaks, see an object, which is usually moving, and look at it. The mother's voice and the movement of the object attract the baby's attention. The mothers' uniform success, in turn, suggests one reason for their belief that the children understand everything. However, we were surprised to find that the mother did not mention the name of the object very often as she requested attention. This suggests that the mother is concentrating on getting the child to attend to the object, and that she pursues only one communicative goal at a time.

In contrast, when mothers try to get children to do things with objects, they are not very successful, except when they give the object to the child. Even in the natural setting children do not appear to understand everything said to them. They are responsive to the speaker, but not necessarily to what she says.

In summary, there is little evidence for extended language comprehension skills on the part of the child in the second year, but there is much evidence that the child responds to the combined effects of movement, and the fact that the mother is saying something to him/her. This responsiveness of the child to the mother's combination of speech and gesture may prove to be an important early indicator of the developing communication skills of the child. Midway in the second year of life, words in the absence of the things and/or actions they refer to will begin to play determining roles in children's responses to speakers.

What Children Say and What They Know

Lois Bloom, Ph.D., Karin Lifter, M. Phil. and John Broughton, Ph.D.

There are currently two ways of describing the relationship between the development of thought and language during the preschool years. One says that the two abilities develop parallel to each other because they are both related to some underlying ability of the child to use language and non-language symbols. The other view is that the two areas develop in a sequence in which language development follows cognitive development. This view holds that language is somehow dependent upon cognitive development. However, a third view is possible in that the developmental relationship between language and cognition may be interdependent, or overlapping, where language and cognition mutually inform one another in development. This means that as children begin to talk, they talk about what they know about objects and events in the world. In turn, as children learn language, they can then use their knowledge of language to learn more about the world.

Early descriptions of children's language dealt with the period in which the child says one word at a time, gradually progressing to the first two-word combinations. These studies showed that the child's language expressed a relatively small number of meanings. The children talked about objects, and the actions on and locations of objects. It was therefore easy to see the connection between the child's language skills and his/her performance on cognitive tasks with demonstrated development of the Piagetian concept of the permanence of objects, since the two main factors which lead the child in this development are the movement and location of objects. As the child progressed in language learning and in sensorimotor intelligence during the second year of life, different kinds of words were identified: those that refer to the names of classes of objects, such as *cookie, doll, chair,* and those that refer generally to the behavior of all objects, such as *more* and *gone.* Knowledge about objects and words develops gradually during the 12 to 24 month period, and gradual changes also develop in the kinds of words learned and used during this period.

Despite these apparent connections between the development of language and thought (specifically, knowledge about objects), many researchers found that performance on tasks related to the concepts of object permanence and spatial relations on standardized test instruments were not good predictors of the language skills of the child. On the contrary, tests of the ability to imitate, and to solve means-end tasks were apparently good predictors of language production.

One important reason why orderly relationships between sensorimotor performance and language performance have not been found is the use of certain scales of sensorimotor development to measure progress in cognitive development. For example, the "Ordinal Scales of Psychological Development" developed by Uzgiris and Hunt is the most comprehensive attempt to date to specify tasks to be used for testing the observations about child development chronicled by Piaget in his "infant books." These scales were designed to be used to assess development, especially so that the developmental effects of different experiences could be studied. However, their emphasis on the effects of differing environmental experiences violates the Piagetian notion of interactions in development, where the child uses developing cognitive structures for interpreting environmental experiences.

In constructing their scale, Uzgiris and Hunt have correctly understood Piaget's description of a universal, unchanging sequence in development, but they have not tried to take into account what the items in the sequence are, nor why there is a sequence that does not change. In Piaget's theory, the stages of development logically follow one another in a regular sequence. Children low in the developmental process have more stages to advance through than those functioning at a higher level.

Testing emphasizes the results of performance on a task. However, it does not take into account the processes of behavior. When behaviors are defined in this way, they are just scored on a simple pass/fail basis. As a result, the way in which the task was solved is ignored. But the child can perform the same task based on different levels of functioning. Therefore, the child's stage of development is reflected in the process of the behavior, and not simply in its results. For example, the discovery by an infant of an object hidden under a cloth (an item on the testing scale) is not conclusive evidence that the child has developed a concept of the existence or permanence of objects. The discovery may be accidental. It is therefore important to look at the way the child solves the task, for example, does the child's behavior indicate that s/he *expects* to find the object hidden under the cloth? Piaget emphasized that what the child learns is the idea that objects are permanent and can be found, and not simply behavioral skills for locating hidden objects. In other words, at any stage in development, the way in which objects are found is qualitatively different from the way this is done at some other stage in development. These changes in the way in which the child does something reflect his/her development of ideas about the world.

There are other ways in which we could evaluate the relationship between thought and language development. For example, the ability to search for objects and to perform reversible actions with objects is basic to both language and cognition. Search is related to the child's ability to have a mental idea of an object, and to his/her ability to search his/her memory for the language forms necessary to understand and to speak. Reversible activity depends upon the capacity to alternate perspective, such as understanding that the relations between objects can be appreciated from different vantage points (for example, taken apart or put together, arranged or unarranged). Such understanding of alternative perspectives is needed for the child to communicate with another person. S/he must alternately comprehend what someone else says, and say something him/herself. Changes in the relationship between such activities as search for objects and performing reversible actions with objects could be evaluated as the child matures.

According to the model of language development described by Bloom, the facts of language are not learned one at a time. Instead, knowledge about objects and aspects of language form, content and use are learned concurrently. Looking at language development in this way encourages us to identify as many factors as possible to account for the developmental relation between thought and language.

Early Patterns of Grammatical Development

David Ingram, Ph.D.

The emergence of the young child's first sentences, and not the first word, may be the most significant early development in verbal communication. This milestone marks the appearance of the unique human ability to formulate grammatical rules of sentence structure.

. Children begin to put words together some time during the second year of life, after several months of single-word speech. Recently, it has been observed that children may vary in how they accomplish this, with regard to rate, phonetic clarity, the rate and nature of spontaneous imitation, and the diversity and type of structures produced. Variation focuses not just on the claim that children are different, but also on ways these differences are manifested, and how behaviors may cluster together. A related topic is the role of cognition, and the importance of individual cognitive skills like mental imagery and imitation for the child's formulation of grammatical rules. By determining the extent to which children differ, we can learn what it is that is shared by all; and by making cognitive comparisons, we should acquire a better understanding of what is particularly unique to the language learning process.

Grammatical productivity and the early emergence of rules of grammar are aspects of early development which underlie research on individual differences and the role of cognition. Productivity refers to that property of rules which allows us to create new instances of structure, so that, for example, a rule that says to put Noun before Verb will place any noun before any verb. In 1979, Ingram described a strict set of criteria for determining whether the individual sentences a child produces are governed by a rule of grammar. In this chapter, a comparison is presented of the early grammatical patterns of two young children both acquiring English as a first language. The two subjects were chosen because they were superficially quite different in their language development and were therefore potential test cases for observing variability in development. In relation to cognitive development, they were at very different stages when sentences first appeared, so that a closer look could suggest those aspects of language development most affected by cognition. Lastly, it was thought that a careful syntactic analysis of their early grammatical rules might reveal different strategies in rule formation, or provide a strong argument for the independence of syntactic (grammatical) development from other aspects of language development.

GRAMMATICAL VARIATION First we can distinguish between syntactic and nonsyntactic variation, the latter referring to those aspects of the child's utterances which do not have to do with the child's grammatical rules. To begin with, there are differences in rate of acquisition, since children do not acquire language at the same speed. In addition, some children imitate spontaneously much more than others. A third nonsyntactic factor is phonetic clarity. Some children produce clear, intelligible speech and are natural candidates for language acquisition studies. Other children, however, may speak quite unclearly and can create problems even for trained linguists. A last nonsyntactic parameter to be considered is the use and degree of babbling. It may be that some children stop babbling at the onset of meaningful speech while others continue to babble while also producing meaningful speech. These four differences are noticeable behaviorally, but it is not clear what they imply for the development of syntax.

The theoretically more interesting aspects of language

development are those that constitute syntactic parameters, such as:

1. Use of presyntactic forms, which are essentially speech sounds without meaning, that are used in combination with meaningful words (such as "[ina] book");

2. Use of free versus rigid word order;

3. Use of general categories versus specific words in rules;

4. Use of memorized formulas versus productive combinations;

5. Breaking down longer utterances into their parts versus putting parts together to structure sentences;

6. Use of diverse grammatical structures and grammatical rules at onset;

7. Use of nouns versus pronouns in referring to objects and people.

Items 3 through 7 constitute the most revealing possibilities regarding grammatical variation. They deal with the grammatical analysis of transcribed and interpreted utterances, and the nature of the rules which govern them. In evaluating the grammatical structure of children's utterances, it is important to remember that an utterance may have a variety of psychological states for the child. For example, the sentence "doggie eat" could be: an unanalyzed whole or an analyzed utterance in which the child knows the words "doggie" and "eat" but has memorized their combination into a sentence. It might also be a partially productive utterance, produced by a rule such as *Agent +* "eat"; or a productive utterance produced by a rule which says that items from the category to which "doggie" belongs may be combined with items from the "eat" category.

Some children may use general categories from the beginning, while others may use more lexically based rules and only build up to general categories. With respect to the use of memorized sentences rather than those produced by rules, it may be that some children express multifaceted information in learned phrases rather than through the use of combinatory rules of grammar. Some children may have rules that produce diverse structures, and others may be limited in this regard. Lastly, there are children who prefer pronouns to nouns in their early word combinations. If children could differ in all of these ways, the diversity would be difficult to cope with. The most complete study of this topic to date, however, concluded that there are two general styles of syntactic acquisition, because of the clustering of some of these behaviors. These two styles are summarized in Table 6, which indicates that the slower learners, the boys, used presyntactic forms, never varied in the use of word order, and were less diverse in the use of grammatical structures. This suggests that they may have been using more memorized formulas or routines. Since presyntactic forms were used by the boys, it may also be that their speech was phonetically less clear. The general impression of these comparisons is that one group of children learned to put together words from different grammmatical categories according to grammatical rules. Their speech was relatively clear with few presyntactic devices. Another group was slower in some cases, less clear and tended to use presyntactic devices that later developed into pronoun forms in multi-word speech.

This chapter presents a more detailed comparison of selected samples of language from two children, a girl K and a boy D. We are interested in determining if their multi-word speech develops in a way predicted by previous studies and, if not, what aspects of their language development correlate with earlier studies. The data collected from K and D showed that K acquired syntax quite early in stage 6 of sensorimotor development, while D, who otherwise advanced similarly to K in cognitive ability, did not use syntax until months later. If the processes of syntactic development are independent of cognitive development, then the grammars of the two children could be potentially quite similar. If, on the other hand, the grammars are influenced by cognition, then D's grammar should show a difference toward greater productivity and generality, since he was not only older but more advanced cognitively at the time syntax emerged in his utterances. Likewise, if

TABLE 6

Summary of Research Data Reported in the Literature[a] on Grammatical Development in Terms of the Occurrence of Eleven Parameters of Variation

Parameters of Variation	Ramer (1976) (4 girls)	Ramer (1976) (3 boys)	Bloom et al (1975) Gia	Bloom et al (1975) Eric	Peters (1977) Minh
		Investigators			
Nonsyntactic					
1. rate of acquisition	rapid	slow	(no differences)		
2. spontaneous imitation					
3. phonetic clarity	(clear?)	(not		not clear	not clear
4. use of babbling		clear?)		yes[b]	
Syntactic					
1. presyntactic forms	few	many	yes		yes
2. variable word order	yes	no	(infrequent)		(no?)
3. type of categories			syntactic	semantic	
4. memorized sentences			(no)		yes
5. phrase processing				(yes?)	yes
6. diversity of rules	diverse	limited			limited
7. mode of reference			nominal	pronominal	

[a]descriptions enclosed in parentheses are those not directly discussed by the authors but apparent from examination of the data.

[b]based on personal communication cited in Peters (1977) p. 569.

syntactic development is independent, when early samples of language from K and D are analyzed grammatically, they should show similar processes of segmentation, combination and categorization, regardless of the cognitive stage at which the particular child is operating. A summary of the cognitive and linguistic development of D and K is given in Table 7.

When the utterances produced by K and D were analyzed, it was found that much of the diversity between the two children was probably due to nonlinguistic factors such as interest in communication, sound play and needs to be understood. In terms of grammatical development,

TABLE 7

Summary of Cognitive and Linguistic Development of
D and K in Terms of Sensorimotor Stages and General
Language Milestones, taken from Ingram (to appear)

D	Sensorimotor Stages	K
	Stage 4	
9-11 mos.		*9-11 mos.*
Acquired no words, but babbled frequently. Appeared to understand "no".		Acquired around 12 words, such as "byebye" "ta", "duck", "mama". Waves when hears "byebye".
	Stage 5	
12-16 mos.		*12-14 mos.*
Favorite babblings are [dadi][mami]. Seems to use "ha" as a greeting. No other words are spoken.		Has acquired over 50 words.
	Late Stage 5, Early Stage 6	
17 mos.		*14-15 mos.*
Says "hi" and also "mami" when wants something. Seems to understand "Daniel" and "no".		Noticeable increase in spontaneous and imitated phrases. Some of the former are "there's a cow", "change the baby", "drop it down".
	Stage 6	
18-19 mos.		*16-18 mos.*
Acquired six or more words at beginning, and starts to show more rapid vocabulary growth.		Multi-word use increased rapidly, and relational patterns emerged.

they were comparable. There is little evidence from this analysis that the additional months of cognitive development for D affected his linguistic development very much. His sentences were somewhat more analytic, yet his categories were neither broader than K's nor his rules more productive.

The onset and acquisition of categories in D's and K's samples indicate that children only gradually acquire categories and the rules which relate them. Children learn to pair sound and meaning in context, and to segment adult speech in the form of sentences into their immediate constituents. The earliest sentences were either memorized wholes or analytic, but little evidence suggested productive rules were being used. The children learned to use certain words with certain others, and stored this information as part of their mental dictionary. Later, as words began to share contexts, broader categories were gradually built up, based on their shared properties. It is proposed that through this gradual procedure, children eventually acquire the categories of the adults' language.

Future research of this sort may determine whether other children begin with greater use of grammatical rules and earlier categories. Certainly it should not be surprising that children rely a great deal on memory and vocabulary. Why should a child use grammatical rules in the first place, except as an efficient way of dealing with an abundance of memorized information? Recent linguistic theory has also turned to vocabulary as an important aspect of language. It is hoped that further elaboration of the kinds of criteria we have used will lead to a greater understanding of the mental grammars of young children.

Clinical Application of the Language and Auditory Milestone Scale

Arnold J. Capute, M.D., Frederick B. Palmer, M.D., Bruce K. Shapiro, M.D., Renee C. Wachtel, M.D. and Pasquale J. Accardo, M.D.

It is important for practicing pediatricians and allied health professionals who evaluate children with developmental disabilities to appreciate the special significance of language development. Language is the best predictor of future intellectual endowment. Its assessment should be the basis of cognitive evaluation in the infant and young child. Language is also the common denominator for the early detection of developmental disabilities. Comparing language development with progress in other developmental areas can yield important diagnostic information.

In comparing the development of an individual child with familiar developmental milestones, two factors should be focused upon: deviancy and dissociation. Deviancy refers to the non-sequential appearance of milestones within a single developmental field (e.g. language) and is valuable as an early indicator of abnormality. Dissociation refers to different rates of progress in separate developmental fields and is helpful in establishing the specific diagnosis. For example, in early infancy, if problem-solving skills are significantly better developed than language, (a language/problem-solving dissociation) the infant is at high risk for a communicative disorder. This may be a peripheral hearing loss requiring careful audiological testing for detection; or it may be a central communicative disorder with abnormal auditory processing which may later manifest itself as a learning disability. Since learning disabilities represent the most common developmental disability, early awareness of language abnormalities allows the professional to identify children at high risk for subsequent learning disabilities.

If the child shows a language/motor dissociation with motor skills significantly behind language abilities, s/he is at high risk for motor delay and possible cerebral palsy. Such a child, at 18 months of age, might have a vocabulary of 12 words (language age: 18 months), plus mature jargoning language (language age: 18 months), but may not be able to sit without support (motor age: 8 months).

There is an urgent need for pediatricians and other professionals to recognize that auditory and language milestones exist and can readily be obtained from parents, particularly the mother, if the professional understands and can interpret them. A series of milestones have been drawn from various sources for use in the language evaluation of handicapped and suspect children at the John F. Kennedy Institute for Handicapped Children in

Baltimore, Maryland. Table 8 lists these language milestones for each month of life for the first 12 months, plus several for the second year, with particular emphasis on the 15th, 18th, 21st and 24th month.

TABLE 8

LINGUISTIC AND AUDITORY MILESTONES*

Language Milestone	Months of Age
1. Alerting	1
2. Social smile	1½
3. Cooing	3
4. Orient to voice	4
5. Orient to bell (looks to side)	5
6. "Ah-goo"	5
7. Razzing	5
8. Babbling	6
9. Orient to bell (looks to side, then up)	7
10. "Da da/ma ma" (inappropriately)	8
11. Gesture	9
12. Orient to bell (turns directly toward bell)	10
13. "Da da/ma ma" (Appropriately)	10
14. One word	11
15. One-step command (with gestures)	12
16. Two words	12
17. Three words	14
18. One-step command (without gestures)	15
19. Four-to-six words	15
20. Immature jargoning	15
21. Seven-to-twenty words	18
22. Mature jargoning	18
23. One body part	18
24. Three body parts	21
25. Two-word combinations	21
26. Five body parts	23
27. Fifty words	24
28. Two word sentences (noun/pronoun inappropriately and verb)	24
29. Pronouns (I, me, you, etc., inappropriately)	24

*1. Permission to reproduce granted by J.B. Lippincott. Reprinted from Clinical Pediatrics, Vol. 17, No. 11, November, 1978. © 1978, J.B. Lippincott Co.

By one month of age, usually within the first week of life, the alerting response (sound recognition) appears and can be detected by a motor response on the part of the infant (for example, blinking, moving a body part, Moro response), or by an increase or decrease in the heart or respiratory rates. Cooing, the production of long vowels, appears at the third month of life. The orienting response, turning the head towards the mother's voice, occurs at 4 months. In addition, there are three other orienting responses elicited by ringing a bell above and to one side of the child's head. The social smile is truly a language milestone and not a social one since it appears at 4 to 6 weeks of life and is not influenced by environmental stimulation.

Gesture language, playing "pat-a-cake" or waving "bye-bye", is a 9-month response. *Dada* used inappropriately usually appears before *mama* even if a father figure is not present in the family. *Dada* and *mama* used appropriately are heard at about 10 months, with a first word appearing at 11 months. The ability to follow a one-step command accompanied by gesture is seen at 12 months of age, and without a gestural cue at 15 months. At this time, four to six words are evident, generally coupled with immature jargoning. (It is important to explain jargoning to parents. Immature jargoning is an attempt at sentence formation using unintelligible speech-like sounds with proper inflection and cadence. To parents, it may sound "like a foreign language".)

At 18 months, there is a 7 to 20 word vocabulary along with mature jargoning, that is, jargoning with an occasional recognizable word. Recognition of one body part also appears at 18 months; followed by three body parts at 21 months, and five body parts at 23 months. By 21 months of age, a two-word phrase is produced. At two years of age, a child usually has at least a 50-word vocabulary and uses two-word sentences. Pronouns (I, me, you) are used inappropriately at this time. Table 9 lists sample questions to ask parents in order to obtain accurate information about the occurrence of these language milestones.

Because these milestones were generated from a vari-

TABLE 9
QUESTIONS FOR OBTAINING ACCURATE
PARENTAL REPORTING OF LANGUAGE ITEMS IN
TABLE 8*

1. When did your infant first recognize the presence of sound by blinking, startling, moving any part of the body, etc.?
2. When did your infant smile at you when you talked to him or stroked his face?
3. When did your infant produce long vowel sounds in a musical fashion?
4. When did your infant turn to you when you spoke to him? (Rule out any visual clues.)
6. When did your infant first say "Ah-goo"?
7. When did your infant first give you the "raspberry"? (Demonstrate.)
8. When did your infant first babble? (Demonstrate.)
10. When did your infant first say "da da" and "ma ma" but inappropriately?
11. When did your infant first wave bye-bye or play pat-a-cake?
13. When did your infant first begin to use "da da" or "ma ma" appropriately?
14. When did your infant say his first word other than "da da" and "ma ma"?
15. When did your infant begin to follow simple commands such as "Give me _____" or "Bring me _____" accompanied by a gesture?
16. (12 months) How large is your child's vocabulary?
17. (14 months) How large is your child's vocabulary?
18. When was your infant able to follow simple commands without any accompanying gesture?
19. (15 months) How large is your child's vocabulary?
20. When did your infant begin to jargon—to run unintelligible "words" together in an attempt to make a "sentence"—or speak as if in a foreign language?
21. (18 months) How large is your child's vocabulary?

22. When did your child's jargoning begin to include several intelligible words?

23. (18 months) How many body parts can your child point to when named? Which ones?

24. (21 months) How many body parts can your child point to when named? Which ones?

25. When did your child start to put two words together? (demonstrate.)

26. (23 months) How many body parts can your child point to when named? Which ones?

27. (24 months) How large is your child's vocabulary?

28. When did your child start to combine a noun or pronoun with a verb?

29. When did your child use three pronouns but inappropriately?

Permission to reproduce granted by J.B. Lippincott. Reprinted from Clinical Pediatrics, *Vol. 17, No. 11, November, 1978.* © *1978, J.B. Lippincott Co.*

ety of different populations at different times by different researchers, further standardization may be necessary. This is particularly important if patterns of deviancy and dissociation are emphasized rather than simply delay in milestone emergence. Standardization data is being collected on normal and handicapped children at the John F. Kennedy Institute. It is anticipated that a questionnaire will develop which can easily be answered by parents, with the assistance of a professional.

Tables 10 - 13 summarize the findings on our first group of 86 Bayley-normal, white, middle-class children. Parents were questioned regarding individual milestones at successive pediatric well-child visits. Two points should be emphasized. First, the individual milestones occur in sequential fashion. The range of variation for each milestone is rather narrow for this group. If this sequential appearance of milestones persists throughout the entire sample of 400 children, the results obtained from the questionnaire procedure should be a good measure of early language development. When refined, the scale can serve as a tool for the early detection and diagnosis of communicative disorders and mental retardation. These milestones are divided into receptive (language comprehension) and expressive (language production) skills. This makes it easier to discern a receptive/expressive dissociation, as is frequently seen in communicative disorders.

TABLE 10
RECEPTIVE PRELINGUISTIC MILESTONES
(0-12 MONTHS)

Milestone	Mean Age in Months	Standard Deviation
Alerting	1.15*	1.54*
Orienting (voice)	3.64	1.20
Orienting (bell)	6.08	1.84
One step command (+ gesture)	11.41	1.78
One step command (− gesture)	13.82	2.36

*Weeks

TABLE 11
EXPRESSIVE PRELINGUISTIC MILESTONES
(0-12 MONTHS)

Milestone	Mean Age in Months	Standard Deviation
Social Smile	4.90*	1.90*
Cooing	6.14*	2.33*
Ah-goo	3.29	1.29
Razzing	4.21	1.58
Babbling	5.83	1.54
Gesture	8.45	1.39
Mama/Dada (inapp)	8.72	1.77
Dada (app)	11.09	2.98
Mama (app)	11.33	2.76
One word	11.15	2.41

*Weeks

TABLE 12

RECEPTIVE LANGUAGE MILESTONES
(12-24 MONTHS)

Milestone	Mean Age in Months	Standard Deviation
One Step Command (+ gesture)	11.41	1.78
One Step Command (− gesture)	13.82	2.36
Five body parts	16.36	2.44
Eight body parts	18.53	2.71

TABLE 13

EXPRESSIVE LANGUAGE MILESTONES
(12-24 MONTHS)

Milestone	Mean Age in Months	Standard Deviation
One word	11.15	2.41
Two words	12.34	2.18
Three words	13.03	2.04
4-6 words	14.32	2.40
Immature jargoning	12.15	2.05
Mature jargoning	16.38	3.03
7-20 words	16.44	3.19
Two-word combination	18.87	2.58
50 words	20.41	2.90
Two word sentences (N + V)	20.67	2.62
Three pronouns (I, me, you, inapp.)	23.07	1.19

In addition to the language milestones described here, the practicing pediatrician and other professionals should become familiar with milestones of articulation (speech production). In the past, since articulation skills do not fully mature until 6 or 7 years of age, speech therapy usually was not initiated until this age. Thus, if a child has a language age of 2 or 3 years, administering formal speech (articulation) therapy would not be indicated, and might even cause frustration to the child, parents and therapist. In this case, language stimulation would be more appropriate than articulation therapy. However, by fully appreciating the existence of these speech production milestones in a child with a language age of 4 to 5 years, articulation therapy can be administered as long as the therapist clearly defines the child's current developmental level. Until the results of further research are available, these articulation milestones can be used as additional clues in identifying deviant or delayed language development.

Clinically, the pediatrician is able to ascertain roughly the level of development of the child's speech production skills by asking the following questions of the parents: At what age was Johnny understood by the immediate family (father, mother, sibling)? The majority of two-year-olds are understood by extended family members (uncles, aunts, cousins). These are valuable clues to the clinician, although only an approximation of articulation ability. Today we realize that children with language disabilities frequently have both delayed language development and delayed articulation development.

Although major efforts are now being directed toward the implementation of habilitation programs, it should be noted that no well-controlled outcome studies conclusively demonstrate a positive effect on development for any habilitation strategy. Such studies are essential and should be a major goal of the 1980's. However, before they can be undertaken, effective methods of early detection and diagnosis in the developing infant must be devised. Attention to prelinguistic and language development in infancy should provide the framework for such early assessment of communication.

Language Development in Handicapped Children

Janet B. Hardy, M.D. and Doris W. Welcher, Ph.D.

The development of language and its associated communication skills of reading, writing and computation is probably the most difficult and complex developmental task facing an individual. It is a task which is more difficult and more critically important in a highly developed technological society than in more primitive ones.

It is believed that language development cannot be considered without also looking at the development of communication skills in general. Language is one of the outputs of a complex neural mechanism, the brain. It is convenient to think of the brain as a very sophisticated computer. The brain, like any good computer, has input channels. These are linked by neural pathways with a central processing unit, which is in turn linked with output channels. The central processor is capable of monitoring and changing output. In general, the better and more complex the "computer", the better will be the quality of its performance. Obvious anatomical or biochemical deficits can cause malfunction.

The potential for development, both physical and cognitive, is established at conception, by the union of genetic material from each parent. As growth and development progress, this potential may be encouraged, or it may be reduced by interactions between the developing child and the many environmental factors to which s/he may be exposed. During intrauterine life, the environmental influences are reduced to biological terms and are mediated through the mother. Birth is potentially traumatic, and the brain is particularly susceptible to damage. After birth, both biological and psychosocial environmental influences directly affect the developing child. The biological influences affect the quality and integrity of the communication system. The psychosocial-environmental influences affect the quality of the programming and input. The ultimate, functional developmental result depends upon the balance between positive and negative effects on the child.

There are a number of biological influences which may affect development. Infection is one of these. Some prenatal viral infections such as rubella may cause mechanical brain damage by the infection and death of vital cells during development. Infection somewhat later in intra-uterine life may lead to more qualitative types of deficits which result in smaller size and number of brain cells due to the generalized infectious process.

There is increasing evidence that nutritional factors during fetal and early postnatal life have important developmental implications. Adequate nutrition is related to infant birthweight, and to later intellectual development. An almost linear relationship exists between an infant's weight at birth and later intellectual functioning measured at 4 and 7 years of age. When birthweight is appropriate for gestational age, the larger the baby at birth, the higher the average IQ score later. This pattern pertains for both black and white children.

The quality of the immediate environment is critical for young children. Important factors are the educational level of the immediate caretakers; the coping ability and the quality of parenting. The results of a number of studies will illustrate these points. During extensive follow-up of approximately 330 children in the Johns Hopkins Rubella Study, it was found that over 60% had hearing defects, 29% had serious intellectual deficits, and only 5% had IQ scores of 110 or higher. Many had a variety of other rubella-related problems including small body size, cardiac defects and visual handicaps. As the children proceeded through elementary school, it became apparent that a high proportion of those with normal intelligence and normal hearing and vision had academic problems consistent with a diagnosis of Minimal Brain Damage.

The children with moderate to severe auditory deficits were identified very early, during the first few months of life. Binaural hearing aids were provided in most cases. Parents were urged to stimulate language development but no outreach services were provided. However, the children were entered into special preschool programs where possible. When they were of appropriate age, they were usually enrolled in special educational programs.

This group of children had problems in communication which could be attributed to difficulty in one or more of the following areas: receiving sound signals; transmitting signals along neural pathways; central processing, storage and retrieval of information; and possibly in initiating output and monitoring that output.

How did these handicapped children fare with respect to language development? The outcome appeared to depend on the basic intellectual capability of the child and the quality of parenting and the parents' ability to cope. Comparing those children with similar intellectual ability and similar handicaps, those who learned language had parents who were highly motivated with respect to language stimulation, kept the hearing aids in repair, and arranged special preschool education for their children. Those who did not learn oral language and depended on sign language were those whose parents did not appreciate the necessity for, or could not provide, these things.

The results of a large child development study and the followup of adolescent mothers and their children provide further insights. The children of adolescent mothers were disproportionately represented among those with perinatal and infant mortality, low birthweight, defective and borderline intellectual functioning, inadequate academic achievement and school failure. In a current Adolescent Program, comprehensive services are provided during the prenatal and delivery periods to about 350 adolescent mothers per year. Approximately half of these mother-child pairs are followed-up and comprehensive services are provided for both mother and child for 3 years. In addition to routine health supervision and well-baby care, family planning services and education are emphasized and intensive instruction is given in parenting, child care, adolescent and child development, nutrition, safety and so forth.

Psychological screening of both mother and baby is routine in the program. The average grade placement of the 13- to 18-year-old mothers is 9.4, although their actual achievement using the Wide Range Achievement Test (WRAT) is much lower. The mothers' receptive vocabulary scores on the Peabody Picture Vocabulary Test show that these mothers are generally disadvantaged in oral receptive vocabulary knowledge.

The children are screened by a psychologist at 12, 24, and 36 months of age. Overall development is generally quite advanced at 12 months. However, language development in terms of vocalizations, imitative behavior and words seems delayed. By age 2 years, overall development for the group has shifted downward, with only 5% achieving above-average scores. At age 3, an even larger proportion is performing in the dull-normal and borderline ranges. At both 2 and 3 years, language development is seriously delayed with greater degrees of delay exhibited at age 3.

Mother-child interaction appears to be a critical factor. Many of the mothers are impatient with their babies. They do not give the babies adequate time for verbal response, nor do they reinforce language performance. They do not usually encourage language development, and their own language provides a poor model for the infant's learning. Having identified these factors, it was found that these young mothers benefit from programs which offer information, role models and understanding.

Delayed language development in early infancy may be a sufficient handicap to impede cognitive development, in general, and to retard academic achievement from the very beginning of the school experience. Intervention programs should begin early in the first year of the child's life with training for better and more stimulating parenthood.

SUGGESTIONS FOR FURTHER READING

Recommended for the non-specialist

GENERAL

*Bower, T.G.R. *A Primer of Infant Development*. San Francisco: W.H. Freeman, 1977.

Bower, T.G.R. *Development in Infancy*. San Francisco: W.H. Freeman, 1974.

*Brazelton, T.B. *Infants and Mothers*. New York: Dell Publishing Co., Inc. 1969.

*Fraiberg, Selma H. *The Magic Years*. New York: Scribners, 1959.

Illingworth, R.S. *Development of the Infant and Young Child, Normal and Abnormal*. Baltimore: Williams & Wilkins, 1970.

*Johnson & Johnson. *Infant Development Program*. New York: Johnson & Johnson, 1977.

*Lewin, R., ed. *Child Alive*. London: Temple Smith, 1975.

Lillywhite, H.S., Young, N.B., and Olmsted, R.W. *Pediatrician's Handbook of Communication Disorders*. Philadelphia: Lea & Febiger, 1970.

Osofsky, J.D., ed. *Handbook of Infant Development*. New York: John Wiley and Sons, 1979.

Sheridan, M.D. *Developmental Progress of Infants and Young Children*. London: Her Majesty's Stationery Office, 1968.

ASSESSMENT

Bayley, N. *Bayley Scales of Infant Development*. New York: The Psychological Corporation, 1969.

Capute, A.J., and Accardo, P.J. Linguistic and Auditory Milestones During the First Two Years of Life. *Clinical Pediatrics*, 17 (1978), p. 847 ff.

Cattell, P. *The Measurement of Intelligence of Infants and Young Children*. New York: The Psychological Corporation, 1940.

Gesell, A., and Amatruda, C. *Developmental Diagnosis.* New York: Paul Hoeber, Inc., 1941.

Uzgiris, I., and Hunt, J. McV. *Assessment in Infancy.* Urbana, IL: University of Illinois Press, 1975.

LANGUAGE AND THOUGHT

Bloom, L. *Language Development.* Cambridge, MA: The MIT Press, 1970.

*De Villiers, Jill G. and Peter A. *Early Language.* Cambridge, MA: Harvard University Press, 1979.

Lock, A., ed. *Action, Gesture and Symbol: The Emergence of Language.* New York: Academic Press, 1978.

Piaget, J., and Inhelder, B. *The Psychology of the Child.* New York: Basic Books, 1969.

Siegel, L. and Brainerd, C. eds. *Alternatives to Piaget.* New York: Academic Press, 1978.

Vygotsky, L.S. *Thought and Language.* Cambridge, MA: The MIT Press, 1962.

NON-VERBAL COMMUNICATION

Adamson, L., Als, H., Tronick, E., and Brazelton, T.B. Social Interaction Between a Sighted Infant and Her Blind Parents. *Journal of the American Academy of Child Psychiatry,* 16 (1977), 194-207.

Als, H., Tronick, E., and Brazelton, T.B. The Achievement of Affective Reciprocity and the Beginnings of Development of Autonomy: The Study of a Blind Infant. *Journal of the American Academy of Child Psychiatry,* 1980.

Brazelton, T.B., Koslowski, B., and Main, M. The Origins of Reciprocity: The Early Mother-Infant Interaction. In M. Lewis and L. Rosenblum, eds. *The Effect of the Infant on Its Caregiver.* New York: John Wiley and Sons, 1974.

Bullowa, M. When Infant and Adult Communicate, How Do They Synchronize Their Behaviors? In Kendon, A., Harris, R.M., and Key, M.R., eds. *Organization of Behavior in Face-to-Face Interaction.* The Hague: Mouton, 1975.

*Chance, P. *Learning Through Play.* Pediatric Round Table 3. New York: Johnson & Johnson Baby Products Company, 1979.

Fogel, A. Temporal Organization in Mother-Infant Interaction. In Schaffer, H.R., ed. *Studies in Mother-Infant Interaction.* New York: Academic Press, 1977.

Fraiberg, S. *Insights From the Blind: Comparative Studies of Blind and Sighted Infants.* New York: Basic Books, 1977.

Massie, H. The Early History of Childhood Psychosis. *Journal of the American Academy of Child Psychiatry,* 14, (1975), 683-708.

Stern D. The Goal and Structure of Mother-Infant Play. *Journal of the American Academy of Child Psychiatry,* 13 (1974), 402-422.

*Thoman, E.B., and Trotter, S., eds. *Social Responsiveness of Infants.* Pediatric Round Table 2. New York: Johnson & Johnson Baby Products Company, 1978.

Tronick, E., Als, H. and Adamson, L. The Structure of Face-to-Face Communicative Interactions. In *Before Speech.* Cambridge, ENG: Cambridge University Press, 1979.

Wolff, P. The Role of Biological Rhythms in Early Psychological Development. *Bulletin of the Menninger Clinic,* 31 (1967), 197-218.

REFLEXES

Capute, A.J., Accardo, P.J., Vining, E.P.G., Rubenstein, J.E., and Harryman, S. *Primitive Reflex Profile.* Baltimore: University Park Press, 1978.

Paine, R.S., Brazelton, T.B., Donovan, D.E., Drorbaugh, J.E., Hubbell, J.P., and Sears, G.M. Evolution of Postural Reflexes in Normal Infants and in the Presence of Chronic Brain Syndromes. *Neurology,* 14 (1964), p. 1036 ff.

SPEECH COMPREHENSION AND PRODUCTION

*Borden, G.J. and Harris, K.S., *Speech Science Primer.* Baltimore: Williams and Wilkins, 1980.

Cohen, L.B. and Salapatek, P., eds. *Infant Perception*. New York: Academic Press, 1975.

Kavanagh, J.F. and Strange, W., eds. *Speech and Language in the Laboratory, School, and Clinic*. Cambridge, MA: The MIT Press, 1978.

Kuhl, P.K. and Miller, J.D. Speech Perception in Early Infancy - Discrimination of Speech-Sound Categories. *Journal of the Acoustical Society of America*, Supplement 1, 58 (1975).

Lass, N.J., Northern, J.L., Yoder, D.E., and McReynolds, LV., eds. *Speech, Language and Hearing*. Philadelphia: W.B. Saunders, in press.

Minifie, F.D. and Lloyd, L.L., eds. *Communicative and Cognitive Abilities—Early Behavioral Assessment*. Baltimore: University Park Press, 1978.

Schiefelbusch, R.L. and Lloyd, L.L., eds. *Language Perspectives: Acquisition, Retardation and Intervention*. Baltimore: University Park Press, 1974.

Smith, S. and Miller, G.A., eds. *The Genesis of Language*. Cambridge, MA: The MIT Press, 1956.

Yendi-Komshian, G., Kavanagh, J., and Ferguson, C., eds. *Child Phonology: Data and Theory*. New York: Academic Press, in press.

COUNTERPART SCIENTIFIC PUBLICATIONS IN THE JOHNSON & JOHNSON BABY PRODUCTS COMPANY PEDIATRIC ROUND TABLE SERIES

Sutton-Smith, Brian, ed. *Play and Learning*. New York: Gardner Press, 1979.

Thoman, Evelyn B., ed. *Origins of the Infant's Social Responsiveness*. Hillsdale, NJ: Lawrence Erlbaum Associates, 1979.

NOTES

NOTES